SEMINAR EDITIONS

231.74
Sö1

1.85

525
08

SEMINAR EDITIONS

Theodore G. Tappert, General Editor

THE NATURE
OF REVELATION

by NATHAN SÖDERBLOM

Edited and with an Introduction by
EDGAR M. CARLSON

Translated by
FREDERIC E. PAMP

FORTRESS PRESS ● PHILADELPHIA

44603

SEMINAR EDITIONS

Christian literature of the past, when read and pondered after the lapse of generations, often sheds new light on the discussion of important questions in our day. Revival of interest in the writings of such diverse figures of the past as Sören Kierkegaard, Blaise Pascal, John Wesley, John Calvin, Martin Luther, Thomas Aquinas, and Augustine (to mention only a few) has served such a function.

Acquaintance with the literature of the past also provides first-hand glimpses into the life and thought of Christians in earlier ages. Men whose names have been encountered in history textbooks take on flesh and blood, and important movements in the history of the church come into clearer focus when the literary deposit of other times is read.

It is the purpose of the present series to make available to the modern reader a number of works which deserve to be better known. Most of them are here translated into English for the first time; the few which were originally written in English have long been out of print. All have been edited with care and furnished with introductions and annotations which will help the reader understand them in their historical context.

The choice of various types of literature—diaries, memoirs, and correspondence as well as theological essays—should add interest to instruction for the general reader as well as the student of church history and the history of Christian thought. The same may be said for the inclusion of European as well as American works.

CONTENTS

INTRODUCTION

Edgar M. Carlson

The reissue of an important work is an act of gratitude and of hope. It is the acknowledgment of a debt to someone whose insight was too seminal and fruitful to be disposed of in a single generation. It is as though one were confessing that there is more to this man than we have digested thus far. Moreover, because of the shortness of memory and the abundance of recent authors, there are many who may not even be aware of a man like Nathan Söderblom. Therefore, it is also an act of hope—hope that a new generation of readers will find themselves addressed, and perhaps enlightened.

The present volume was first published in 1903, reissued by the author in 1930, and translated into English in 1932. The original publication contained only the single essay which carries the title "The Religion of Revelation." The second edition included two additional essays on related themes, "The Portals of Revelation" and "Continued Revelation," which were also included in the English translation. The 1930 edition carried a brief preface in which Söderblom acknowledged that he had often been requested to issue a new edition and had yielded to these requests on the ground "that the book as originally written had gained a significance for the study of the history of religion and ought therefore to be made available with as little change as possible." The

1932 English edition has also long been out of print and there have been continuing requests for it. The one hundredth anniversary of the birth of Nathan Söderblom in 1866 provides an excellent occasion for meeting those requests as well as for honoring the contribution of one of the great Christian thinkers and leaders of this century.

While a centennial observance may be an adequate reason for publishing a book, it is not necessarily an adequate reason for reading it. And this is a book that deserves to be read, not only to satisfy historical curiosity or antiquarian interest but for the very substantial personal enrichment which it may be expected to yield.

The history of thought is not accurately depicted if one thinks of it as a level plane on which proponents and adversaries engage in combat and either demolish one another or negotiate a truce which allows for some middle ground. Philosophical and theological systems are not generally "vanquished." They lose attention and adherents because they do not speak to the situation in which the listeners find themselves, or because attention is distracted elsewhere. One set of ideas seems pertinent in a given situation and it becomes fertile and grows. It gains an able exponent and he develops a following. Then another pattern of ideas may appear, without necessary connection to what has gone before; with an able exponent it may become a lively and dynamic element in the thought world. The validity and relevance of each does not seem to depend on the thoroughness with which any preceding position has been demolished.

Often the stimulus for such a new direction comes out of the rediscovery of an earlier student and his work. One could cite, for instance, the way Kierkegaard influenced a wide variety of schools of thought separated from him by several generations; or even more dramatically, the way the rediscovery of Luther vitalized twentieth-century theology. The student of culture, not least in its religious aspects, can never content himself with "the latest works." They are likely to reflect the conditions of the times so completely that they offer little perspective for analysis and appraisal. They are governed by the contemporary debate and do not lead us beyond it. It is a wholesome exercise for the student to immerse himself in a vital and germinal work out of another era. He thus becomes involved in another debate in which he can be more objective. The setting in which it occurs is not identical with his own time, although it may well have helped shape it. To work one's way through a volume like this one, and to try to put oneself into the setting of the time that produced it can be a very helpful and fruitful exercise.

Fortunately, we are here dealing with a very facile pen in the hand of an exceedingly clear thinker. At certain points he may go further than the reader cares to follow, but his thought is clear and incisive, and his writing is inviting. Moreover, he is a bright and scintillating spirit whose warmth and congeniality shine through his scholarship. His capacity for appreciation was enormous and the breadth of his talents was great. He loved music and felt that Bach represented perfection in this art. On the other hand, when he broke into song in the midst of a sermon, as he did on occasion, not infrequently it would be in the words of a pietistic revival hymn. He mastered rare languages in order to study religions first-hand, notably Parseeism. His studies covered the historical, biblical, and systematic fields in religion. He was at home in philosophy, and in his expositions of mysticism he increasingly made use of psychological ideas and theories. He was the kind of thoroughly sensitive and broadly informed specialist in the field of the history of religions who might well serve as a model for the modern scholar in any field.

The above paragraphs may suggest that one would do well to read this book just to get acquainted with the mind of Nathan Söderblom. But there are also additional reasons for reading it. Surely one of the frontiers for Christian thought today is the relation of Christian and non-Christian religions. Ecumenicity has reached the level where it seems in good conscience to extend to the boundaries of the Christian community of believers. Söderblom would have loved to see this day. He is most commonly referred to among his Swedish disciples and in wider circles as "the ecumenical church father." He contributed significantly to the understanding of differences within Christendom and sought ways to bridge those differences, but he was already deeply concerned about the whole realm of religion in all its forms. We may very well find here helpful guidelines in reaching a Christian understanding of world religions. The need for such understanding grows more urgent every day.

Futhermore, Söderblom is important for the understanding of the very significant contemporary theological developments in Sweden. It is widely recognized that some very important research has been done by Swedish theological scholars during the present century and that some very important findings have emerged. Best known are Anders Nygren's investigations of *agape* and *eros* as basic motifs in Christian history and Gustaf Aulén's espousal of the classic *Christus Victor* interpretation of the atonement. The method of "motif research" has been exceedingly fruitful and the historic-systematic approach has yielded a large body of historical research and systematic analysis. Söderblom is recognized as one of the two key figures in this twentieth-century development. He and Einar Billing are the twin pillars that form the gateway into this fruitful era. They raised crucial questions and set the pattern and direction for subsequent theological research. The study of this little volume is therefore at the same time an introduction to a large body of important theological literature.[1]

[1] For more extended descriptions of this theological development see Nels Ferré, *Swedish Contributions to Modern Theology* (New York: Harper, 1939), and Edgar M. Carlson, *The Reinterpretation of Luther* (Philadelphia: Westminster, 1948). There is now available in English a rather large number of works which is representative of this theological production, including the following: Anders Nygren, *Agape and Eros*, trans. Philip S. Watson (London: S.P.C.K., and Philadelphia: Westminster, 1953); Nygren (ed.), *This Is the Church*, trans. Carl C. Rasmussen (Philadelphia: Muhlenberg, 1952); Nygren, *Christ and His Church*, trans. Alan Carlsten (Philadelphia: Westminster, 1956). Gustaf Aulén, *The Faith of the Christian Church*, trans. Eric H. Wahlstrom and G. Everett

INTRODUCTION

Nathan Söderblom 1866-1931

Nathan Söderblom was born January 15, 1866, in Trönö parish in the province of Hälsingland, where his father, Jonas Söderblom, was then serving as pastor. He is said to have received his great gift of intellect, his exceptional energy, and his intense personal devotion, marked by pietistic emphases, from his father; from his mother he received those qualities of warm friendliness and marked empathy which made him one of the most congenial and deeply loved men of his generation. There was in him a remarkable combination of graciousness, personal piety, exceptional intellectual powers, and almost unlimited energy. The impact which Söderblom made upon his own country and upon the world —sufficient to earn him the Nobel Peace Prize in 1930—was the impact of an exceptional leader of men as well as an outstanding scholar in a field of study.

He began his studies at Uppsala in 1883 and took his first degree *(fil. kand.)* in 1886. At that time he was inclined to pursue studies in classical philology but after a brief period of indecision entered upon the study of theology. He took his theological degree in 1892 and was ordained the following year. In 1890 he visited the United States to participate in a student Christian conference at Northfield, Massachusetts. Thus began his long identification with ecumenical activities. He there made the acquaintance of John R. Mott, with whom he was to work closely and for whom he always entertained the very highest regard. Söderblom became a leader in the Student Christian Movement in these early years. There is some evidence that his activities and ideas were regarded with suspicion among certain conservative segments of the Swedish clergy.

Arden (Philadelphia: Muhlenberg, 1948; 2nd ed.; 1960); *Christus Victor,* trans. A. G. Hebert (London: S.P.C.K., 1931); *Church, Law and Society* (New York: Scribner's, 1948). Gustaf Wingren, *Luther on Vocation,* trans. Carl C. Rasmussen (Philadelphia: Muhlenberg, 1957); *The Living Word,* trans. Victor C. Pogue (Philadelphia: Muhlenberg, 1960; paperback, 1965); *Theology in Conflict: Nygren, Barth, Bultmann,* trans. Eric H. Wahlstrom (Philadelphia: Muhlenberg, 1958).

It may have been criticism of these "radical tendencies" that led Archbishop Sundberg in 1894 to offer him the post of legations pastor in Paris as well as seamen's pastor in the ports of Dunkerque, Calais, and Boulogna. He accepted the appointment and, after his marriage to Anna Forsell (to whom this volume is dedicated), transferred his activities to Paris. There he spent seven very important years. He became acquainted with the Swedish colony of artists and developed aesthetic interests which made him a life-long friend of the arts and of artists. Most important, he continued his studies at the Sorbonne, specializing in the history of religions and their interpretation and comparison. His period of study coincided with heightened interest on the part of scholars in the whole field of world religions, and he found himself stimulated by the vast new bodies of information now made available in this field. He concentrated on Parseeism and during his Paris years published two volumes growing out of this research, the first entitled *Les Fravashis* (1899) and the second, his doctoral dissertation, entitled *La vie future d'après le Mazdéisme* (1901). On the basis of the first volume, he was nominated as a successor to C.P. Tiele, at Leyden, one of the acknowledged luminaries in the field of world religions.[2] During this same period he also published a volume entitled *Jesu bergspredikan och vår tid* ("Jesus' Sermon on the Mount and Our Time") which is of particular interest because it indicated the extent to which Söderblom was influenced by Albrecht Ritschl and some of the respects in which he found Ritschl to be deficient.

In 1901 Söderblom was named professor of "theological presuppositions and theological encyclopedics" at Uppsala University. The appointment was one which allowed him considerable latitude, and he was able to range broadly over the historical, systematic, biblical, and philosophical fields. His research was continuous and his production impressive. It is out of those early years that *The*

---

[2] Söderblom later reworked Tiele's monumental *Kompendium der Religionsgeschichte* (originally published in 1880), apparently on Tiele's recommendation.

Nature of Revelation comes.[3] His reputation in the history of religions led to invitations to go to Berlin to establish a chair in that field in 1911 and another invitation from Leipzig shortly thereafter. After making arrangements which permitted him to retain his Uppsala professorship, he accepted the Leipzig appointment. Although he was there only a year, the brief tenure served to cement relationships with many European scholars, including Adolph Harnack, Ludwig Ihmels, Rudolf Kittel, Adolph Deissmann, and others.

In 1913 the archiepiscopal chair became vacant with the death of J. A. Eckman, who had been Söderblom's predecessor at Uppsala. It is the practice in Sweden for the clergy to nominate three candidates from which the king appoints one. Söderblom received the third largest number of votes but was given the appointment. He was thus called upon to terminate his formal academic career, but his research and writing continued at an amazing rate.[4] Many of his writings were scholarly works in the field of the history of religions, such as *Gudtronsuppkomst* ("Origin of the Belief in God"; 1914), *Ur religionens historia* ("Out of the History of Religions"; 1915), and, of course, the Gifford Lectures of 1931 bearing the title *The Living God*.[5] It is indicative of the level of his scholarship that he could retain leadership in his field through all the years of his archbishopric sufficient to warrant the prestigious appointment as Gifford lecturer. During these same years he also developed his interest in Luther research and in 1919

[3] As originally published it contained only the first chapter, and this in a somewhat abbreviated form. It appeared under the title "Uppenbarelsereligion" ("The Religion of Revelation") in *Skrifter i teologisk och kyrkliga ämnen tillägn. C. A. Thorén* (Uppsala, 1903), pp. 199-253, and was subsequently printed separately.
[4] A comprehensive bibliography of Söderblom's published works is found in *Nathan Söderblom in Memoriam*, ed. Nils Karlstrom (Stockholm: Svenska kyrkans diakonistyrelses bokförlag, 1931), pp. 391-451. The bibliography lists 669 titles between the years 1889 and 1931. They cover a very wide range of subjects and appeal to very different audiences. It is noteworthy that many appeared in the daily press. However, there are several dozen works that represent very substantial productions, many of them several hundred pages in length.
[5] This volume is available in a paperback edition published by Beacon Press (Boston, 1962). It contains the biographical introduction by Yngve Brilioth as published in the original Oxford University Press edition of 1933.

THE NATURE OF REVELATION

published *Humor och melankoli och andra Lutherstudier* ("Humor and Melancholy and Other Luther Studies") and in 1922 *Tre livsformer* ("Three Patterns of Life"). The war years reveal the extent to which Söderblom grappled with problems related to church and state and his effort to see the church contribute significantly to the resolution of the world's problems. Out of this experience seems to have come the urgency of his concern with Christian unity which received its most concrete expression in the Stockholm Conference on Life and Work in 1925. This same concern is evidenced also in numerous publications, including *Christian Fellowship*, which was published in the United States as part of the "Christian unity handbook series."[6]

The Stockholm Conference was almost solely the product of Söderblom's initiative and energy. It was one of the major impulses toward cooperative thought and action among the Christian churches and took concrete form as the Life and Work movement which united with Faith and Order in 1948 to form the World Council of Churches. The conference also established Söderblom as an ecumenical leader whose parish became the world. His already large circle of friends and acquaintances was further enlarged, not only within Christendom but among leaders of other world religions as well. His interest in mysticism, for instance, had as its consequence close personal associations with Sadhu Sundar Singh and Tagore of India.[7]

Despite his research and writing and the heavy demands of his ecumenical activities, his conscientious fulfillment of his duties as primate of the Church of Sweden claimed his first loyalty, and he is remembered for his indefatigable travels and his innumerable sermons and addresses in every part of the country. It is said that he "catechized" not only the confirmation classes but the congrega-

[6] *Christian Fellowship or the United Life and Work of Christendom* (Chicago: Fleming H. Revell, 1923).

[7] The book *Tre Livsformer* (Stockholm: Hugo Gerbers förlag, 1922) uses Sundar Singh as the example of one kind of mysticism, and although he distinguishes it from "trust," of which Luther is the example, he gives it the sympathetic chapter heading "Evangelical Mysticism in an Indian Soul."

tions. His interest was pastoral to the end. He died on July 12, 1931, and lies buried in Uppsala Cathedral.

Söderblom's Theological Contribution

Even before Söderblom's death his theological contribution was being appraised and analyzed. Gustaf Aulén, on the occasion of Söderblom's sixtieth birthday, published a paper entitled "Nathan Söderblom and Contemporary Swedish Theology."[8] Aulén observes that the turn of the century marked a dividing line in Swedish theology. During the nineteenth century Swedish theology was submissive to and dependent on major schools of thought elsewhere, especially in Germany. During the present century, Swedish theology has had a relatively independent development. It cannot be aligned with any side in the shifting theological fashions elsewhere. This change, said Aulén, was in good part the product of Söderblom's creative and highly provocative insights and the research out of which they came. Aulén would credit Einar Billing with another major share in this development.[9]

It was Söderblom's "universal perspective" which led Swedish theology out of its isolation. He was interested in and informed about the whole gamut of religious experience and expression. But this universality, notes Aulén, was coupled with a marvelous cer-

[8] Gustaf Aulén, "Nathan Söderblom och nutida svensk teologi," *Svenska teologiska kvartalsskrift*, I (1926), 3-19.

[9] Einar Billing is little known in the United States except for a very small volume *Our Calling*, trans. Conrad Bergendoff ("Facet Books—Social Ethics Series," No. 1; Philadelphia: Fortress, 1965). His influence on Swedish theology was probably greater than that of Söderblom. His theological production was not large but it pioneered in new directions. Among his more provocative works may be mentioned his essays on ethical thought in primitive Christianity, *De etiska tankarna i urkristendomen i deras samband med dess religiösa tro* (2nd enlarged ed.; Stockholm and Uppsala, 1936); his doctoral thesis on Luther's teaching on the state, *Luthers lära om staten i dess samband med hans reformatoriska grundtankar och med tidigare kyrkliga läror* (Uppsala: Almqvist & Wiksells boktryckeri, 1900); and his essay on the atonement, *Försoningen* (Stockholm: Almqvist & Wiksell, 1908). In each of these Billing opened up new approaches to the understanding of the Christian faith which were fruitful in subsequent Swedish theological development. See Conrad Bergendoff's essay, "The Ethical Thought of Einar Billing," in Philip J. Hefner (ed.), *The Scope of Grace* (Philadelphia: Fortress, 1964), pp. 281-306.

tainty concerning the genuinely Christian and evangelical. There was in him none of that "naive universalism" which is without any criterion for judging and "therefore allows the darkness to make all cats black."[10] His concern for the essentially Christian in faith and life motivated his study of Luther as well as his study of religions generally.

At the time of Söderblom's death Aulén again offered an analysis of his theological achievement in an extended chapter in *Nathan Söderblom In Memoriam*.[11] Here he becomes more specific in identifying the contributions which Söderblom made to Swedish theology. He lists five influences. 1. Söderblom provided some of the main concepts which have become characteristic of Swedish theology and some of the major impulses which have subsequently borne rich fruit. 2. His anti-doctrinaire and unbiased approach to religion in general and Christianity in particular created a favorable climate for research and creative thought. 3. He had a genius for discerning the genuine and was impatient with mere formalism. 4. He was able to see beyond form to content and thus was able "to penetrate through the shell into the kernel of the matter." 5. He gave Swedish theology a sense of independence and self-consciousness. He was himself a blend or synthesis of the national and the international. He was more in touch with and more sensitive to influences from other parts of the world than any other Swedish theologian and yet none was more characteristically Swedish than he.[12]

If Söderblom's total effect on Swedish theology was in the direction of giving it a character of its own, it was due in part to the scope of his contacts elsewhere and to his engagement with the broader theological currents of his time. Thus, it is of interest that among his very first publications should have been a translation and reworking of a French interpretation of Ritschl's view of

[10] Aulén, "Nathan Söderblom och nutida svensk teologi," p. 8.
[11] Aulén, "Den teologiska gärningen," *Nathan Söderblom in Memoriam*, pp. 63-104.
[12] *Ibid*., p. 75.

Christianity.[13] He acknowledged strong influences from Ritschl, especially in his early years, and continued to speak of him with respect and gratitude when his own theological position had diverged sharply from that which characterized Ritschl. What was especially important is that Ritschl helped Söderblom to see the relation between revelation and history, thus severing the characteristic association between theology and speculative philosophy. Söderblom called attention to the christocentric emphasis in Ritschl's theology and it seems evident that this had a lasting influence. It is generally acknowledged that Ritschl influenced him also in his study of Luther. The concentration upon history as the matrix out of which religious knowledge comes gave to religious personalities immersed in history a particular relevance. But the significance of Söderblom's theological contribution is to be found, nonetheless, at the points where he came to conclusions that differed sharply from those of Ritschl. Thus Ritschl had ruled out mysticism as a valid approach to religious knowledge; Söderblom described all religion in terms of types of mysticism. Ritschl had shown little interest in the church and had focused attention on the kingdom of God and the ethical demands on the inner life; Söderblom not only loved the church in the concrete form in which he encountered it but found it to be integral to the whole idea of revelation. Ritschl had ruled out eschatology, whereas Söderblom felt that concern for the ultimate outcome of history was inherent in revealed religion. It was one of the criteria by which the basic forms of religion could be distinguished. Tor Andrae is undoubtedly right when he asserts with regard to Söderblom's total theological production that "his thought, both as to structure and content, has little in common with Ritschl."[14] The framework and context of Söderblom's theol-

[13] Published under the title *Ritschls åskådning af kristendomen: Ernest Bertrands Une nouvelle conception de la redemption, livre premier*, trans. and reworked by Nathan Söderblom (Stockholm: P. A. Norstedt & Söners förlag, 1893). The introduction Söderblom provided is highly appreciative of Ritschl, and somewhat defensive.

[14] Tor Andrae, "Nathan Söderblom som religionshistoriker," in *Nathan Söderblom in Memoriam*, p. 50.

ogy is not Ritschlian; even when he uses Ritschlian language and ideas they do not mean the same because they appear in a different setting. While Söderblom was in some respects the most Ritschlian of the Swedish theologians of the opening decades of the present century, it is as the one who transcended and overcame Ritschlianism that he left his mark on Sweden and on the world.

Söderblom makes relatively few references to Schleiermacher but it is clear that there was much in Schleiermacher's "religious consciousness" which is congenial to Söderblom's discussion of mysticism and the intuitive apprehension of religious reality. He was a close friend of Baron von Hügel and there are clear traces of the baron's influence upon him. In his later years, Söderblom seems to have been attracted to Henri Bergson, and this association may be reflected in his growing interest in the metaphysical aspects of reality and its expression in theology.[15]

Söderblom's associations with Roman Catholic scholars may be of particular interest to the modern reader. He was sufficiently at home in the field of Roman Catholic scholarship so that he could give an admirable analysis of what was then "Roman Catholic modernism" in his *Religionsproblemet inom katolicism och protestantismen* ("The Religious Problem in Catholicism and Protestantism"), published in 1910. It is significant that when Söderblom referred to "the crisis in Luther research" he was referring to the reappraisal of Catholic scholars such as Imbart de la Tour (who asserted that Luther had gone overboard in the direction of mysticism) rather than to the new directions which had been taken by Karl Holl and others in Germany.[16]

While Söderblom was open to influences from all directions there was nothing eclectic about him. All that came to him was transformed and vitalized by the fertile and imaginative mind

---

[15] Aulén reports that in his last conversation with Söderblom, shortly before his death, the archbishop spoke of the risk of setting theology free from all metaphysics. Aulén, "Nathan Söderblom och Einar Billing—kontraster i samverkan," *Svenska teologiska kvartalsskrift*, XXXVIII (1962), 212.

[16] *Tre Livsformer* (Stockholm: Hugo Gerbers förlag, 1922), pp. 92-94.

through which it passed. He could take what was old and discarded by his contemporaries, such as apocalyptic and dualistic elements, and make it speak to current issues. There were no established forms into which new insights and new knowledge needed to be crammed. There was nothing sectarian or partisan about either his life or his thought. He seemed to have unbounded confidence that God was at work revealing himself in life and learning and that one need not be afraid of what research in either would bring. This openness was balanced by an unusual sense of commitment to God, the church, and the gospel. In his sermon at Söderblom's funeral, Einar Billing, his long time associate and friend, referred to him as the "man of simple obedience."[17]

There are two problems which constitute part of the background of Söderblom's thought and which still concern us today. They are (1) the implications for faith of historical-critical biblical research and (2) the aggressively naturalistic world-view. Söderblom describes the anxiety which he experienced over biblical criticism as parallel to Luther's *terrores conscientiae*. Aulén quotes him thus: "For us it was not something inherited or bought at a bargain, but a revelation from God himself, when the issue of the truth of Christianity was shifted from the question of the errorless book and letter to God's living revelation in history, fulfilled in Jesus Christ and continued in each human soul to whom grace has been granted. Over the Scriptures fell a new light."[18] Aulén observes that both Söderblom and Billing worked with these "problem-complexes" and that it was characteristic of both of them that they came to a view of revelation relevant to both of the problems. That which was liberating in reference to historical-critical biblical research brought with it an understanding of history and nature which was liberating in reference to the assertions and pretensions of a naturalistic world-view. The historical-critical method not only posed problems for both men but gave them unexpected help as

[17] The Swedish phrase is *en den enkla lydnadens och pliktuppfyllelsens man* (*In Memoriam*, p. 3).
[18] Aulén, "Nathan Söderblom och Einar Billing," p. 208.

well. Neither seems to have been inclined to circumscribe the application of scientific method to the biblical materials. Both of them turned to the history of religions, in addition to their own exegetical studies, for understanding the nature of religion and the distinctive character of Christianity. While biblical studies were not Billing's specialty, he made extensive use of their findings in developing his own highly original and fruitful interpretation of the Old and New Testaments.[19]

Söderblom's contributions to the science of the history of religions are many,[20] and it would be quite possible to incorporate much of his work under this category. For instance, his analysis of types of mysticism took Luther, Loyola, Erasmus, and Sundar Singh as examples. This could clearly be regarded as a contribution to the study of the history of religions and their varied forms. However, Söderblom's interest was also, and equally, systematic. It is probably more accurate to say that Söderblom used his knowledge of the history of religions and of the types of religious experience and apprehension as materials which were useful in the interpretation of the Christian message and mission.

Aulén identifies five centers of interest around which Söderblom's research and theological production clustered. They are (1) the question of revelation, (2) the problem of the church, (3) Luther research, (4) the cross, and (5) the ecumenical problem.[21] We shall consider each of these in turn.

The Question of Revelation

The Nature of Revelation is the best single source for understanding Söderblom's total theological position. Yngve Brilioth, himself a distinguished scholar and later archbishop of Sweden, writes in the introduction to the Gifford Lectures, *The Living God*, concerning this publication, "We here meet *in nuce* many of the trends of thought which in an amplified form occur later in his

---

[19] See his *De etiska tankarna.*
[20] See the bibliography in *Nathan Söderblom in Memoriam.*
[21] *In Memoriam,* pp. 76-104.

writings, not least in this volume of the Gifford Lectures."[22] He identifies these more specifically as "the energetic insistence upon the religious life as a separate province of experience, not to be identified with the moral; the distinction between prophetic religions, which go back to a personal founder, and the religions of 'nature and culture'; between the 'mysticism of the infinite' and the 'mysticism of personal life.'"

This volume was originally intended as a contribution to the "Bible-Babel controversy" which was triggered by discoveries dealing with Babylonian and Assyrian religions and their parallels in the history of Israel. It was specifically an interpretation of these from the pen of Friedrich Delitzsch to which Söderblom addresses the introductory pages of the original edition in 1903. The translator properly felt that these were not germane to the argument of the book and omitted them. The larger and enduring question raised by the controversy is the relation between religion and culture, particularly as the question is confronted in the religion of the Old and New Testaments and its relationship to the larger cultural setting of the Hebrew people. Söderblom gives it as his judgment that the discussion would not have been so disturbing and confusing if "unevangelical and theologically obsolete theories of literal infallibility and an unhistorical, mechanical concept of revelation had not been permitted to frighten us away from each new bit of knowledge and to turn over revelation's own weapons to the enemy, and if it had not been considered smart to withhold from the congregations insights which cannot be denied and which are not intended to weaken or disturb the Christian faith."[23]

What Söderblom is undertaking to do then is to set forth a view of revelation which is not subject to this limitation. He makes the bold assertion that no religion is a product of culture; all religion depends on revelation. Then he proceeds to utilize the materials of his research in the history of religions to develop patterns which

---

[22] *The Living God,* p. xviii.
[23] Quoted from the Swedish edition of 1930, pp. 9, 10. These pages are among those that were deleted in translation.

have identifiable distinguishing marks. He finds that there are two major kinds of religion which he identifies as "nature" or "culture" religions on the one hand, and "revealed" religion on the other. The distinction is not absolute since revelation is involved in all religion and all religion is affected by culture. But the relation between religion and culture is not such that the higher culture always possesses the higher religion. The reverse may be true. Söderblom has a highly illuminating analysis of how culture religion develops under the influence of developing social structures, leading to polytheism with a hierarchy of government, and is then dissipated into pantheism, idealism, or agnosticism. Significantly, this cycle never produces a genuine monotheism.

The exceptions to this are Zoroaster's Ahura-Mazda and Israel's Jahweh. One of the very original and intriguing aspects of Söderblom's analysis is the parallelism between these two. He was a recognized authority in the Zoroastrian religion and used his intimate knowledge of it to elucidate the distinctiveness of Christianity. The reader will be impressed by the crucial role assigned to Moses in this analysis, as well as the contribution of the prophets.

The study of the history of religions as it was pursued in the early decades of the century tended to focus on parallels and similarities. It developed comprehensive, generalized concepts of religion within which all religions could be incorporated. Thus the distinctiveness of each tended to be dissolved in the common characteristics. Söderblom had a genius for allowing his materials to develop their own patterns. Tor Andrae says, in commenting on this, that there are two types of researchers. One masters the materials, applies to them logical analysis, and puts them into established categories. The other is mastered by the object being studied and approaches the material intuitively. "For Söderblom nothing is more characteristic than his intuitive understanding, his unusual ability to lay hold, quickly, surely, and incisively, on the essential in a wide and varied field of research."[24]

There is much which suggests the evolutionary hypothesis in the

[24] *In Memoriam*, pp. 28, 29.

view of revelation which Söderblom unfolds, but if one attempts to correlate it with such a view one will be disappointed. Indeed, Söderblom consciously challenges the view of Christianity which holds that it is "the flower of the development of religion, its final end, into which all the different lines of general revelation have converged." It will not fit into that framework. Most religion has evaporated into abstraction; it has not developed into anything even remotely resembling Christanity.

It is not the purpose of this introduction to serve as a substitute for the reading of the volume. This would be to shortchange the reader. Let me suggest, however, that the reader observe how the two kinds of religion are differentiated by their varied reactions to history, to eschatology, to nature, and to dualism. Note how the distinction between "revealed" religion and "culture" religion becomes the distinction between the "mysticism of personality" and the "mysticism of infinity," and how these can be further defined by characteristic marks.

The two types of mysticism are to be found in the Christian tradition and have correlative ethical viewpoints, but Söderblom clearly believes that the one represents the "deeper furrow" and the more authentic embodiment and expression of what is essential and distinctive in Christian faith and life.

When *The Nature of Revelation* was reissued in 1930 two additional essays were joined to it. One, first published in 1910, carries the title "The Portals of Revelation." What Söderblom is dealing with here is the reception of revelation, its apprehension as a genuine element in experience. This is, of course, the other side of any revelatory process. He is concerned to assert that revelation involves a genuine knowledge of the essential nature of reality, of God. Here one can recognize a kind of empiricism and existentialism. Reason does not provide the materials of revelation. The primary portals of religious apprehension are intuition—with its concomitant of feeling—and conscience with its urge toward perfection. It is the function of reason to organize, systematize, and control the patterns of expression, but it does not itself produce the materials with which it works. There is genuine religious knowledge gained through the "intuition of infinity," and some persons are more sensitive than others. Jesus becomes the example, par excellence, of the urge to perfection, and therefore the unequaled revealer of God. If one is tempted to write this off as mere moralism one will be misunderstanding Söderblom's intention.

There is a highly suggestive comparison of the method of science and the revelatory interpretation of nature and history as two planes which can be superimposed upon existence. Science applies the category of causality and gathers up that which can be arranged in a causal continuity and which is useful for the purpose of adapting nature to our needs and purposes. Revelation calls us to wrestle with reality itself in order to catch its inner meaning.

The other addition which was made to the original essay when it was reprinted in 1930 carried the title "Continued Revelation." It was originally published in 1911 with the title *Ett bidrag till den kristna uppenbarelsetrons tolkning* ("A Contribution to the Interpretation of the Belief in Revelation"). It was immediately considered to be a work of great importance. Here Söderblom asserts that it is not possible to establish the fact of revelation at all unless one assumes that it continues to the present time.

One must bear in mind that for Söderblom revelation is not a narrow concept but includes what has been traditionally described as "general revelation" as well as the more restrictive "special revelation." It may thus have the elemental meaning of that which is given, one's heredity, as compared to character which is in some measure the product of one's reaction to life. The genius is a channel for revelation in this general sense. His counterpart in the moral and religious realm is the thoroughly committed man through whom God is able to act in unique and distinctive ways. There is a strain in Söderblom's thought that is reminiscent of the hero idea in Carlyle (whom he quotes). For that matter, it is equally reminiscent of Luther.

In spite of Söderblom's irenic attitude toward Roman Catholicism, he does not hestitate to distinguish sharply between what Rome means by "continued revelation" and his own understanding of it, which is both more mundane and more daring. It is interesting and instructive to observe how freely he incorporated secular forces and ideas into a theological view of existence. One has the feeling that Söderblom would have much to contribute to the present discussion of the task of theology as it is understood by the "theological secularists."

This does not represent any blurring of the genuinely religious and the distinctively Christian. It is precisely "the re-creation of the individual human being" which is at the center of Söderblom's view of revelation, and this has a strongly ethical character. The reader will note how Söderblom consciously draws on Kant and Wilhelm Herrmann in his understanding of conscience and of how it is liberated. He will note, too, how the grand sweep of God's revelation is concentrated in the engagement of the individual soul with the gospel. The history of God's dealings in the past becomes a history of God's dealings with the individual.

The above analysis suggests some of the riches to be found in this modest volume. Hopefully, it also indicates how relevant it is to the current theological discussion.

The Problem of the Church

Söderblom was a devoted churchman who not only gave distinguished leadership to the Church of Sweden during his time as archbishop but also helped to develop deeper currents of self-understanding within it through his interpretation of its nature and role. Along with Einar Billing he was responsible for the so-called "Young Churchmen's Movement," which gave considerable vitality to the folk-church concept in the early decades of this century. He linked it with his conception of the continuing revelation, which he understood to take place in the total life of the church rather than through the hierarchy as in Roman Catholic theology. He was fond of pointing out the continuity which characterized the Swedish church from the medieval period through the Reformation and to the present. This, he said, was typical of its nonsectarian character. He regarded the inclusiveness of the folk-church as admirably suited to declare and depict the universality of God's grace. He emphasized its relationship to the total culture while insisting on the uniquely religious function and mission of the church. He insisted, too, on the integral relation between the forgiveness of sins and service in one's calling. The church integral to the nation was the coordinate of faith integral to one's total vocation. While it was Einar Billing who gave the classic statement of this relationship, it is reflected in all of Söderblom's writings concerning the church.[25]

Söderblom himself acknowledged indebtedness to Ritschl with respect to his understanding of the church, and it is certain that he found something liberating and expansive in Ritschl's emphasis upon "the kingdom of God." But it is clear that the term had more specifically religious content for Söderblom than for Ritschl, who tended to understand it primarily in ethical terms. The theology of Ritschl did not elsewhere produce the sort of respect for and devotion to the church which was characteristic of Söderblom. Indeed, in many instances it tended toward individualism and disassociation from the church.

Luther Research

Almost everything that Söderblom wrote bears evidence of his deep interest in Luther. It may not be necessary to account for this by any outside influences, since one of the very earliest manuscripts from the young Söderblom's pen had to do with Luther. It is generally assumed, however, that Ritschl's influence was a factor in encouraging him to pursue this interest. Since history was the only

[25] Cf. Billing, *Our Calling.* Among the better known works of Söderblom expressing his views of the church are *Svenska kyrkans kropp och själ* ("The Swedish Church's Body and Soul"), published in 1915 (Stockholm: P. A. Norstedt & Söners förlag), and *Den Enskilde och kyrkan* ("The Individual and the Church"), which appeared in 1909 (Uppsala: L. Norblads bokhandel).

valid source of religious knowledge for Ritschl, the New Testament era and the Reformation period became special foci of attention. However, in Söderblom the inquiry took a decidedly different turn than one might have expected, and one which would not fit into Ritschl's pattern. Söderblom seems to have been interested in Luther's inner life as much as in its external expression or its conceptual form. He gave Luther an honored place among the great mystics. He was the pattern and exemplar of the classic and authentic mystical tradition to which he gave various names—"personality-mysticism," "will-mysticism," "spontaneous mysticism." Ritschl had no confidence in any kind of mystical experience. Someone has remarked that Ritschl led Söderblom to Luther and Luther led Söderblom away from Ritschl. This may very well have been the case.

The major product of Söderblom's interest in Luther was the volume *Humor och melankoli och andra Lutherstudier*, which appeared in 1919.[26] This is a very distinctive approach to Luther and his theology. Söderblom's purpose is not solely to analyze Luther's theology or to recount the historical data related to him. The work does not fall into the historical-systematic approach which has characterized Swedish Luther research during the present century,[27] although it contains elements of it. There is a psychological aspect involved also. One might say that Söderblom examines Luther as he examines other evidence related to the history of religions. He is attracted to the clearest and most impressive embodi-

[26] *Humor och melankoli och andra lutherstudier* (Uppsala: Sveriges kristliga studentrörelse skrift serie, 1919).

[27] The method of "motif research" (*motif-forskning*) combines the historical and systematic approaches and seeks to identify the affirmation of faith which is contained in the varying forms of expression. Under changing circumstances the same affirmation may appear in different dress and may be concerned to counteract a different error which would compromise or obscure it. The search for the basic motif is a search for the central affirmation in the light of which all other affirmations must be understood. Billing's theological method was "historical-systematic," while Söderblom's might more accurately be described as "historical-psychological." Aulén and Nygren developed and refined the method of "motif research" but they freely acknowledge their indebtedness to both Billing and Söderblom.

ment, in thought and life, of a religious position and then seeks to understand the phenomenon. Luther is not only an exponent of a theological interpretation; he is also a case in point, an instance of religious expression.

As such, Luther is a paradox. On the one hand, we encounter a sense of humor which seemed entirely uninhibited; on the other hand, anxiety and melancholy which have some of the marks of pathological experience and behavior. Söderblom makes quite an extensive survey of instances of humor in Luther and identifies its characteristic marks. He notes that while Luther's humor was sometimes coarse, it was never bitter. His humor was a sort of safety valve for his inner tension, which would otherwise have been unendurable. But the most important thing is that there is a correlation between the fact of his humor and the lack of legalism in his understanding of the Christian way. His central religious conception of God's grace, freely offered, prevented rancor and bitterness from entering into Luther's humor, and his humor helped him to understand and clarify his central religious principle. It helped him to break with the cultivated asceticism or patterned mysticism which is generally the product of deep religious concern and commitment. Luther brought about a change in the "life ideal" inasmuch as he released the believer from a patterned piety prescribed by the church or the monastic order. Luther's conception of grace and of the direct personal confrontation of each man with God made the prescribed patterns of piety which he had encountered in the monastery inappropriate and even impossible. The heart must belong to God, and each life must be formed by this central allegiance, but how it is formed depends on the circumstances and upon the person's own nature. Holiness cannot be standardized. Söderblom considers it noteworthy that the other reformers tended to stamp a pattern on their followers, such as puritanism, and he believes that this can be explained by the fact that none of the other reformers possessed a sense of humor. They were therefore not able to break through the ascetic, prescribed forms of piety.

They were not able to take the equality of all callings with complete seriousness.

Of course, if one means by "humorist" the total reaction of a man's life to existence Luther could not qualify as a humorist. Söderblom thinks only those who view life as observers, such as playwrights, can be humorists in this sense. The prophetic experience involves men in personal suffering and in sharing the sufferings of others. Humor is not, therefore, the primary response. "Luther's humor is a ray of sunlight that pierces profound darkness."[28]

The larger portion of the volume is devoted to Luther's melancholy. We have here one of the most extensive and sympathetic investigations ever made of those experiences in Luther's life which are referred to by the term *terrores conscientiae*. Söderblom tries to trace the history of Luther's melancholy, to analyze it in psychological as well as theological terms, and to appraise its bearing on his theological position. It is very unfortunate that this volume is not available in English. It offers quite an unusual contribution to our understanding of Luther as an exceedingly sensitive person with almost impossible inner tensions, which must have aggravated his own problems but which undoubtedly also drove him forward to a more unequivocal understanding of God's free grace than would otherwise have been possible. Söderblom, however, distinguishes between the feeling of anxiety and the sense of guilt. It would be a mistake, he thinks, to equate these in any way. If this had been the case, Luther should have been relieved of his anxiety and melancholy when he found the evangelical assurance through which he found release from guilt. The more serious vexations come after he has left the cloister, however, indeed after he has taken his stand for justification through faith. Sometimes these periods of anxiety and travail were accompanied by physical ailments. Often he accomplished an amazing amount of work simultaneously with these attacks.[29]

[28] *Humor och melankoli,* p. 67.
[29] Söderblom develops much the same analysis of Luther's anxiety in *Tre Livsformer.* There he says Luther understood the difference between moral evil

The practical deduction which Söderblom makes from his studies of Luther's melancholy is that Luther found help for this personal problem in and through his understanding of the gospel, even though it was not specifically a religious problem. Modern man may be more conscious of other problems, such as meaninglessness, emptiness, or futility, than he is of guilt. Luther would have understood such problems and would have considered that the gospel was addressed also to these. For him, however, there would have been no evident need for distinguishing between what is religious and what is not, since he saw all of life as being involved in a common need and finding its healing in God's unmeasured love.

In the setting of this psychological and theological investigation Söderblom uncovers at least two elements in Luther of which he made extensive use elsewhere. One is the spontaneity of the believer's response to the gospel. All patterned piety is rejected. The new man is liberated at the center of his being. The decisive action is the inner struggle. When God has taken a man's heart captive, his life is free. The other element is the dualistic pattern in Luther. The struggle that took place in Luther's inner life was to him a struggle between God and the devil. This is more than theological ornamentation; it relates to the basic structure of his thought. Söderblom had of course already become aware of the importance of dualism in distinguishing between religions and in the interpretation of the New Testament. We have also noted the correlative emphasis in Parseeism, with which Söderblom had become intimately acquainted.

Frequently Söderblom employed the method of contrast to delineate the types of mysticism and to clarify his own interpretation of

---

(*das Böse*) and want or deprivation (*das Uebel*) but for him they merged into one. This, Söderblom thinks, makes Luther more modern since it is commonly asserted that the modern man is more conscious of want than he is of guilt. "The religious problem arose for him not solely out of the needs of conscience but equally out of the needs of life. Melancholy signified for Luther the hardships of human existence in as intense a form as possible. Luther has a message for him who is without peace through no fault of his own, as much as for the person who suffers the agonies of a guilty conscience" (p. 73).

the faith. Thus there is a very interesting comparison of Erasmus, Luther, and Loyola in *Christian Fellowship*, in which each is viewed as a continuation of the medieval church. Erasmus, thinks Söderblom, is the only one of the three who may be properly described as a reformer. The other two "were impelled by a deeper pathos, an all-consuming desire for peace of soul. They found it in different ways, and each in his way forms an original religious type. It may be disputed which is the straighter way, that which continues through Luther, or that which continues through Ignatius Loyola and Tridentinum."[30] Erasmus is the representative of religion under the influence of culture, governed by an ideal of what the church should be and devoted to improving the church in the light of that ideal. Söderblom suggests that the best example of the Erasmian influence is the Church of England.

Luther and Loyola were more intense than Erasmus; they had experienced "heaven and hell." Both were rooted in medieval mysticism and moved beyond it. Loyola took the course of methodical self-training and self-discipline as a means toward the ecstatic experience and subjected the mystical training of the soul entirely to the discipline of the church. He thus moved beyond medievalism in his patterned piety. Luther, on the other hand found the answer to his need in the grace and pardon of God which generate faith and trust and which lead the believer to faithful fulfillment of his earthly calling.

Söderblom regards both Luther and Loyola as genuine mystics. He says that "Luther belongs to medieval mysticism in the same way that St. Paul belongs to Pharisaism."[31] They both consider the only good to be union with God, but they conceive of that union in different ways. For Loyola the way is cultivated, disciplined, calculated. For Luther everything is spontaneous, uncultivated, and unforced. God is too immediately present and his presence is too overwhelming to contain the divine energy in clearly fixed channels.

[30] *Christian Fellowship*, p. 46.
[31] *Ibid.*, p. 60.

It will be noted that in this description Luther becomes the pattern of a type of mysticism which Söderblom designates as "spontaneous mysticism" or the "mysticism of spontaneity" (*spontan mystik*). Loyola, on the other hand, is the exemplar of "cultivated mysticism" (*övnings mystik*).

The Centrality of the Cross

When Aulén makes this one of the major foci of Söderblom's theological production he is making a comment about the man as well as about his ideas. It is possible to find evidence of a growing concentration on the cross in Söderblom's theological exposition, but one has the feeling that this reflects personal need as well as the inherent demands of a system of theology. Indeed, it would be erroneous to interpret Söderblom's theology at any point as a construct of the mind apart from a confession of the heart. He had no hesitation about using that kind of language. His most extended commentary on the meaning of the cross is his *Kristi pinas historia* ("Christ's Passion History").[32] Written in 1928, it reflects the maturity of his experience as well as his scholarship. It is a book of devotion as well as a genuinely scholarly work.[33] Fortunately, one chapter of this volume is available in English bearing the title *The Mystery of the Cross*.[34]

It will also be clear that Söderblom's analysis of Luther, and especially his focus upon the *terrores conscientiae*, moves in this

[32] *Kristi pinas historia* (Stockholm: Svenska kyrkans diakonistyrelses bokförlag, 1929).

[33] Aulén says about this book, "This is not one of those books which is written because there should be a book on the subject. Every page in it witnesses to the fact that it has been a concern of the heart for the author. *Kristi pinas historia* is from many points of view a very remarkable book, filled throughout with the author's varied and penetrating knowledge, looking out in all directions upon the religions of the world, and still in the fullest sense of the word a book of devotion which speaks about Christianity's central mystery incisively and with classical simplicity, elucidating it from a wide variety of points of view, but allowing it, nonetheless, to remain what it is, a mystery." *In Memoriam*, p. 98.

[34] *The Mystery of the Cross*, trans. A. G. Hebert (Milwaukee: Morehouse, 1933).

same direction. Few persons have interpreted Luther's inner anguish as sympathetically as he or found as rich theological implications in it.

Aulén observes that Söderblom's concentration upon the cross came to be especially noticeable after World War I. God's relation to the suffering of the world was a personal problem for him, and he became convinced that God is involved in it. This was clearly the implication of the view of revelation which he had expounded in the original 1903 essay on revelation. God reveals himself in history; this is the distinctive mark of revealed religion. Therefore, God is inevitably involved in suffering. Theologically, this means that suffering penetrates the very being of God. In its most intense form, this problem is faced in the person of Christ, and especially in his death. It will be recalled also that Söderblom allowed a very important role to the exceptional personality and that one of the characteristic marks of the mysticism of personality is the role of the authoritative personality. This kind of personality is also the example without parallel of the revelatory significance of "the urge to the ideal." All of these strands in Söderblom's thought lead him to the central fact in the proclamation of the gospel, namely, Christ's vicarious death. In the same way, the more clear it became to Söderblom that forgiveness is the essence of the gospel and of the Christian understanding of love, the larger loomed the significance of the cross.

In the volume before us there are some splendid passages comparing the two types of mysticism with respect to the interpretation which each makes of man's essential need. There is "the outstretched hand, a longing, dreaming gaze," which characterizes the mysticism of infinity, and the "man who shrinks back in dread and dares not even lift up his eyes" because he can only plead for mercy, which is the characteristic mark of the mysticism of personality. To be sure, there is at least one instance of a religion which belongs to the mysticism of infinity but yet concerns itself with evil. That is Hinduism. But Hinduism reacts to evil by fleeing from existence. It accepts the inevitability of evil in the very nature of existence and seeks to escape from existence into the totality of being, where all individuality is lost. There one no longer finds either nature or history.

The Ecumenical Task

Söderblom was the author and editor of the Swedish edition of the report on the Stockholm Conference on Life and Work in 1925.[35] It included nearly a dozen contributions by Söderblom, all of them related specifically to the ecumenical task. But the theological presuppositions of his ecumenical outlook are apparent in what has been said throughout this introduction. The interest in the history and comparison of religions, and the imaginative and creative manner in which he allowed them to speak for themselves as well as his restraint in judging them; the inclusiveness of the patterns of religious faith and life within which he worked and the broad sympathy which he had for all; the driving interest in the characteristically Christian with the absence of any sectarian narrowness; the breadth and depth of his view of revelation and its dynamic and contemporary quality—all these dictated an ecumenical view of the church and of the gospel. It would be a mistake to assume that Söderblom felt "life and work" to be the substance of Christianity or that he regarded it as more important than "faith and order." On the contrary, Söderblom wrote as early as 1916 *(Svenska kyrkans kropp och själ)* against any attempt to achieve an inclusive church by combining the values of each of the churches and seeking to cooperate in externals only. What is required is that each church shall be aware of its distinctive gifts and combine faithfulness to its own with respect for others.

[35] *Kristenhetens möte i Stockholm augusti 1925* (Stockholm: Svenska kyrkans diakonstyrelses bokförlag, 1926). The English report of the Stockholm Conference was prepared by G. K. A. Bell, then dean of Canterbury, under the title *The Stockholm Conference 1925: the Official Report of the Universal Christian Conference on Life and Work held in Stockholm, 19-30 August, 1925* (Oxford University Press, 1926).

The Church of Sweden became aware of its own ecumenical character under the guidance of Söderblom and Einar Billing. "The religiously motivated folk-church" became an attractive idea to many who responded by their participation in the "Young Churchmen's Movement." Since it could serve as the home for a great variety of religious confessions and expressions, it seemed reasonable to suppose that the various Christian communions could similarly live together in spite of their differences.

While Söderblom and Billing provided the premises for an ecumenical view of the church, one does not find in them a formal "theology of the church." It was a spirit which they breathed into the church life of their nation and their time. Söderblom's example and leadership were, of course, more important than any careful analysis or well developed rationale could have been, at least as far as its effect upon the Swedish church is concerned. Aulén and Nygren and others have provided more formal and systematic presentations of a doctrine of the church.[36]

An Assessment

How has Söderblom's theology fared during these years and what are its prospects now? Those who were in contact with Lutheran theological education in the United States prior to Söderblom's death are almost certain to have encountered considerable skepticism concerning him. He did not fit the "orthodox" patterns, and to the extent that these still held sway Söderblom was looked upon with suspicion. He would have been described by the terms "liberal," "modernist," "Ritschlian," and sometimes in stronger language. Outside of Lutheran circles in this country there was undoubtedly a good deal of awareness of the man but few would have had much access to his thought. Practically all of his works

[36] For example, Aulén, *Till belysning af den lutherska kyrkoidén, dess historia och dess värde* (Uppsala: Almqvist & Wiksell, 1912) ("Toward the Elucidation of the Lutheran Idea of the Church, Its History and Its Value"); or Anders Nygren (ed.), *This Is the Church*.

that have appeared in English came out shortly after his death. In academic circles he was acknowledged as an authority in the history of religions, and this was much more the case in Europe. As a theologian, Söderblom has enjoyed respect but his influence has been modest in North America.

One of the reasons for this is that another generation of Swedish scholars, many of whom were influenced and stimulated by him, moved ahead of him and attracted widespread attention. Gustaf Aulén, who was associated with him at Uppsala for seven years, is frequently referred to as Söderblom's "disciple." He moved to Lund in 1913, and the center of theological research in Sweden was transferred to that university. The so-called Lundensian school gradually came into being with such names as Aulén, Anders Nygren, Ragnar Bring, Gustaf Wingren, and others. Söderblom, like Billing, was tremendously important to this development, and Swedish theologians freely acknowledge their indebtedness to him. Others are less aware of it. Söderblom the historian of religions is relatively well-known, but Söderblom the theologian is not.

Are his ideas pertinent and viable in today's thought world? It is hazardous to predict, of course, but as one works through his thought there is no accompanying sense of being distant from the contemporary debate. On the contrary, the questions of theological methodology, the translation of religious concepts into more general categories, the analyses of the religious consciousness and its history—these all seem to this observer to be extremely promising aids for realistic and creative engagement on some very contemporary fronts.

There has been at least one very thorough critique of Söderblom's theology to which reference should be made. It is a work by Folke Holmstrom entitled *Uppenbarelsereligion och mystik—en undersökning av Nathan Söderblom's teologi* ("The Religion of Revelation and Mysticism—An Investigation of Nathan Söderblom's Theology").[37] It is a rather involved analysis of the varieties

[37] Stockholm: Svenska kyrkans diakonistyrelses bokförlag, 1937.

of mysticism and the categories in which they are described. Holmstrom believes that there is a "psychological mainline" and a "psychological sideline" and an "essential mainline"[38] and a "practical-pedagogical sideline" between which Söderblom oscillates. Chronologically, Söderblom tends to move from a distinction in principle to a psychological distinction. Holmstrom argues that in *The Nature of Revelation* Söderblom arrived at a distinction between the mysticism of infinity and the mysticism of personality, which is a distinction in principle. It is substantive and relates to the meaning of Christianity. But in the Gifford Lectures, *The Living God*, he makes distinctions on the basis of psychological factors which are not related to or dependent on the distinction in principle. These he refers to as "will-mysticism" and "feeling-mysticism" or "spontaneity-mysticism" and "cultivated mysticism." These latter terms refer to psychological types rather than to distinctive positions or patterns of doctrine. They are subjective rather than substantive. This shift enables Söderblom to bring together widely different interpretations of the gospel. For instance, it allows him to compare Loyola and Luther without making any judgment as to the authenticity of the religion of each. In effect, says Holmstron, Söderblom deserted the difference in principle in the interests of greater universality in the concept of the church. It would take us afield to investigate the evidence which is adduced in support of this criticism. But we have taken note of it so that the reader may bring it with him into the reading as a counterfoil which may help in the analysis of the pages that follow.

* * *

The original English translation carried an introduction by Edward Caldwell Moore which was highly appreciative of this volume but which has not seemed germane to its reissue at this time. However, the fact that it is being brought out again offers confirmation of Professor Moore's judgment: "I am convinced that this is a work of high importance to those who would give account

[38] The Swedish is *principiel hufvud-linje.*

to themselves of their own religious convictions or who would have a share in the shaping of an adequate theology."

The translator's note to the English translation reveals that he had access to a copy of the Swedish edition in which Söderblom "had made with his own hand a number of changes and also included additional material. This will explain the differences in the text which may be noted by those familiar with the Swedish original." We have assumed, therefore, that divergences from the original may be accounted for by changes made by the author. A few minor changes in the translation have been made with the permission of the translator and the publisher.

The bibliographical information in Söderblom's original footnotes would have identified the works cited for the readers of that day; since many of these works are unfamiliar today it was felt necessary to provide further publication data. Such information, insofar as it was available, has been supplied by the editor; all material in brackets has also been supplied by the editor.

Those who find that the reading of this volume stimulates an appetite for more may wish to seek out the following volumes by Söderblom which are available in English:

Christian Fellowship or The United Life and Work of Christendom (Chicago: Revell, 1923).

The Mystery of the Cross, trans. A. G. Hebert (Milwaukee: Morehouse, 1933).

The Living God, Basic Forms of Personal Religion (London: Oxford University Press, 1933; reissued Boston: Beacon Press, 1962).

Hastings' *Encyclopedia of Religion and Ethics* (1956 ed.) has seven articles by Söderblom: "Ages of the World" (Zoroastrian), "Ardashir I, Asceticism" (Persian), "Communion with Deity" (introd., Parsi), "Creed" (Parsi), "Death and Disposal of the Dead" (Parsi), "Holiness" (General and Primitive), "Incarnation" (introd., Parsi).

Works about Söderblom include the following:

Peter Katz, *Nathan Söderblom, a Prophet of Christian Unity* (London: G. Clarke, 1949); this consists of selections from the memorial writings of Bishop Berggrav, Bishop Brilioth, Bishop Andrae, and others, with an introduction by the Bishop of Chichester.

Hugh G. G. Herklots, *Nathan Söderblom, Apostle of Christian Unity* (London: SCM Press, 1948).

THE NATURE

OF REVELATION

by NATHAN SÖDERBLOM

To

Anna Söderblom

née Forsell

PREFACE

The little book *The Nature of Revelation (Uppenbarelsere-ligion)* has for many years been out of print. There has been much demand for it and I have often been requested to issue a new edition. I have delayed doing so because I intended to include its essential contents in some work of larger dimensions. It has, how-ever, been urged, rightfully I think, that the book as originally written had gained a significance for the study of the history of reli-gion and ought therefore to be made available with as little change as possible. It is herewith presented in a revised edition. I have made a few improvements and minor changes. To the original article have been added two of later date, which treat of the same subject from different points of view.

NATHAN SÖDERBLOM

September 24, 1930

1

THE RELIGION OF REVELATION

Some Points of View

I

In the discussion as to the merits of different religions and the superiority of one to another, the common standard has been the ethical. One religion is superior to another because it has a better ethical code. In such a comparison the religion of Israel has nothing to fear. It is not, however, by its ethical elevation that a religion is proved superior, although a higher moral code will ultimately be found to accompany that which constitutes the essential superiority of a religion. A comparison of the ethical content of one religion with another cannot give a true *religious* valuation. Religion is not a "thou shalt," and its value is not to be measured by the development which it has reached in ethical relations between man and man. On the contrary, in religion we seek help and life. What does it profit a man if he possess the most excellent worldly wisdom and knowledge of human nature, the best ethical code, yes, even the most beautiful ideals, if faith and hope collapse, if heaven is closed and the spiritual sun of divine power and love is darkened, so that the spirit is left cold and empty? A lofty, severe, and sensitive morality, without religion, beautiful and admirable though it may be, is nevertheless nothing but poverty. In comparison with it, however, religion without morality is a shameless pretension, riches which the holder does not possess. The human soul cannot live on morality alone. It must have religion, it must have faith. Harald

Höffding,[1] in his philosophy of religion, has sought to reduce to lowest terms that support for life which man seeks in religion. He has certainly carried the reduction to a minimum when he holds that religion is faith in the persistence of values. But even in this minimum definition, which is evidently inspired by the theory of the conservation of energy and which offers less than the least possible, rather than the reverse, there is contained this truth, that the value of a religion is measured by its ability to give victorious confidence, to guarantee value and meaning to life if this be lived in accordance with its truth. No comparison of moral injunctions can give a true valuation of the religions with which they are historically more or less associated.

Most certainly we must take morals into account in the study and valuation of a religion, and this in two respects. First, with respect to the character of the morals. Second, and this is more fundamental, with respect to the nature of the connection which the religion in question has with the moral life. First and last a religion must be judged by its religious resources. It is impossible to understand the religion of Israel and to see its place in the history of religion without taking the religious point of view. In the nature of things, it is self-evident that the ultimate valuation must be upon the question of the religious power possessed by a religion. This truth has certainly not been accepted and applied in our day. The traditional and, on the whole, undisputed principle is to make the ethical the decisive standard in the history of religions, and to arrange and value religions according to their moral code. No one would dispute the tremendous significance of this principle and its close connection with the question of religious power. But it is not the point of view of religion itself. For the final question put to religion is not: "How will you shape my life, what ought my life to

---

[1] [Höffding (1843-1931) was a Danish philosopher of considerable repute in the Scandinavian countries and beyond. He was influenced by Kierkegaard in his earlier years but developed a rather distinctive philosophy of value. This was worked out especially in his *Philosophy of Religion* (1901). He argued that the real strength in religion is its belief in the persistence of values beyond the borders of experience.]

be?" It is rather this: "How can you rescue my life and sustain it, so that I may not be engulfed in a meaningless existence or lost in despair?" The latter question cannot, however, be separated from the former.

Eduard Geismar[2] has uttered a timely word, not without a pointed paradox which I would include, when he wrote concerning Old Testament religion: "Let it remain there, that element of egoism; therein lies the elevating power of revelation. The strength of Israel is not in an exalted morality; its strength is in its religion, in its faith. There is no greater misrepresentation of the history of Israel than to force it into the modern conception of religion in which religion must be an appendix to morals."

Do morals then lie deeper in human life than religion, so that religion must be based on morals if it is to secure an essential place in life at all? Is morality the only certain thing in the spiritual world, so that religion must draw the certainty of its reality from morals, if it is to have any such at all? It is a persistent, but nevertheless a mistaken conception, that the roots of morality go deeper down and spread more widely in human life than the roots of religion. Religion stands by itself both in history and in the life of the soul. If anything can be said to have been established by scientific inquiry concerning religion in the past century it is the insight that the ground and nature of religion can as little be satisfactorily explained by locating it in the will as by locating it in the intellect, although it must find expression both in the will and intellect. Neither can it be explained, in the customary triple division of the faculties of man into intellect, will, and emotion, by referring it to the emotions, although its role in the emotional life is an exceedingly important one. The roots of religion lie deeper, in its own central organ in man, in the spirit. Pascal calls this center "the heart." Schleiermacher made the matter clear in his *Reden*. He reveals that the place where religion lives its own and essential life

---

[2] [Eduard Geismar was a Danish theologian and philosopher (1871-1939). He was Professor of Ethics at the University of Copenhagen. Among his better known works are two volumes on Sören Kierkegaard.]

is in the very innermost center of the personal life of the individual, where the divine and eternal life is mirrored in a fountain which lies in the deepest depths of the soul, if only that mirror is undimmed. The same experience and insight, which in the science of religion is bound up with the name of Schleiermacher, is found on closer examination, under different terms and in spite of great differences, in all the great and earnest thinkers concerning religion, not only within but also outside of the biblical religions. The center of religion in the life of the human being is in the spirit. Man is, according to Rudolph Eucken, the meeting place of different sorts and degrees of reality.

II

If we compare Babel and Bible from the religious point of view, there is apparent a difference between them, which becomes more marked and assumes a more comprehensive importance as we view the history of religion as a whole. This difference can perhaps best be expressed by making a distinction between nature-religion and culture-religion, on the one hand, and prophetic religion on the other. The uniqueness of the prophetic religion I would characterize by giving it the name of revealed religion.

The two terms revealed religion and culture-religion require an explanation before we enter upon a discussion of the difference which I have indicated.

1. The word "revelation" is used in this connection in a special sense. A revelation of God is present wherever a real religion is found. Where God is known, it may be even imperfectly and through a distorting medium, there he has in some degree allowed himself to become known, yes, made himself known. The two other interpretations generally offered, to explain the fact of the existence of religious faith and truth outside the biblical revelation, break down completely. Are all cases of piety and virtue outside the Christian revelation simply a work of the devil, a caricature perpetrated

by demons, as we may read in Augustine? How then can they be true, and in important respects similar to those of the Christian faith? Mohammed believed that the Jinns by stealth were able to snatch up what was said in heaven. (The Koran, 37:7 ff., and other passages.) Or, if the truth about God, which is found in the religions apart from those of the Bible, be the product of man's own reason, as has been taught all the way from the apologists of the early church down to the various theories of "natural religion," where shall we draw the line between the divine and the human in the religions of the Bible? Justin, with his sympathy for Greek philosophy and his doctrine of the *logos spermatikos*, the divine Word sown as a seed (*sperma*) throughout humanity, and Tatian, proud of being a barbarian and despising the Greeks, represent two constant lines of thought in Christian apologetics. Could a comparable faith in divine providence, a comparable religious seriousness and pious practical wisdom in Socrates, or Seneca, or Epictetus be a devilish deception or a self-discovered wisdom, but a work of God in the psalmist or in Paul or Tertullian? Nay, belief in a general revelation of God is forced upon us, so soon as we make a serious acquaintance with non-Christian religion, even where this shows itself debased, degraded, or "ignorant" (Eph. 4:18), and however loudly it may call for the gospel of the cross. Ultimately all certainty of God and divine matters has its source in an intuitive sense of God. We must concede that Troeltsch and Gunkel and all the younger theologians are right when they demand that we take seriously faith in a general revelation of God. *No religion is a product of culture*, all religion depends on a revelation.

This is an ancient Christian idea. Partly because of the exclusively theological point of view which has characterized different lines of thought in the past century, and partly because of our lack of acquaintance with the literature and spiritual treasure of the ancient world, we have lost some of the fresh, immediate, and uplifting feeling, so strong in our older theologians, that it was the same God, our God, who held Socrates "on the watch-tower, where we have been set and which we ought never of our own will to leave," firm against the temptation of suicide; that it was the same God who met Seneca "wherever he turned," of whom he knew that "He sustained all things" and that "He is not worshipped with the fattened carcasses of slaughtered oxen nor with gold and silver nor with money which is cast into the treasury, but with a pious and sincere will," and with prayer: "Pray for a sincere heart, for the health of the soul first and then of the body, pray to God with boldness." It was the same God, our God, who gave to Epictetus his strong, humble confidence: "Just that which happens I choose as best; I am satisfied with my fate; for I consider that which God wills better than that which I will. To him I would bind myself in love as a good servant and a faithful slave; his wish, his desire shall be mine; in short, his will be mine!" If this feeling were alive now, we should find sympathy even in ecclesiastical circles with the prayer of Nebuchadnezzar to Marduk:

A ruler who wishes to obey thee am I; the work of thy hands am I.
It is thou who hast created me, and
Thou hast entrusted to me the lordship over humanity,
According to the mercy which thou dost show to all.
Grant that I may love thy high guidance!
Implant in my heart fear of thy Divinity!
Grant to me what seemeth good to thee, for it is thou who hast the
  lordship over my life.

or with the plaintive cry to Ishtar:

I, thy servant, pray with sighs unto thee,
Thou, who dost hear the earnest prayer of the sinner,
Thou, whose glance giveth man life.
O, thou Almighty One, Queen of the nations,
Thou, the merciful One, who doth turn in mercy and receivest the
  petitions of those who pray.

Enthusiasm for the elevated and powerful elements found in the Babylonian and Assyrian expressions of piety constitutes a reaction against that narrow view which has gone with the over-valuation of the truth-content of the biblical revelation, such as has been prevalent during the past century. Even pagans have known that "we are also his offspring." They have been "feeling after him."[3] And "he has not let himself be without witness."[4] We ought to read Origen's interpretation of such texts. It is high time, in this age of world missions and world communications and the final flow of world history in one deep stream, that the church acquaint itself with the thought of the general revelation of God.

2. This is one side of the matter. On the other side we note that every higher religion demands as a necessary condition a certain measure of culture. This includes the religion of prophecy. No phenomenon in the history of religions, no revelation has sprung forth as a *deus ex machina* without the given cultural conditions. We shall return to this theme later, and discuss it in greater detail.

The terms culture and revelation cannot, however, be conceived as mutually exclusive. In the area of history there are, generally speaking, no forces or movements which are totally exclusive. But this does not mean that we must not rightfully and necessarily distinguish the different nuances which emerge in history.

This brings us to the principal and most significant distinction which the history of religion has to present. This distinction is not one that cuts sharply across the threads of development where a new woof in the weaving begins. Rather it is a cut lengthwise along the warping of the weave. This distinction reaches back as far as we can see anything clearly in the history of Israel from the time of Moses, but it includes also certain phenomena outside the limits of Israel.

In the first attempt to construct a philosophy of the history of religion, on the basis of a richer and more complete knowledge of

[3] [Acts 17:27-28.]
[4] [Acts 14:17.]

this history, C. P. Tiele has set up "the law of the spiritual unity of man" and applied it to the relation of the religious development to that of the general culture. This principle is insofar true that a higher culture cannot in the long run fail to influence religion. But if we mean thereby that the general development of the spirit of man in culture, in the conquest of nature, in social structure, in science, art, and morals is matched by that of its religion, so that the higher religion follows the higher culture, religion and general culture appearing side by side in their progress through their different epochs and principal forms, the principle will not hold good. Or rather, it divides the history of religion into two unequal parts, one of which corroborates the law of the spiritual unity of the race, and the other radically contradicts that law.

Let us take a hurried view of that part of the history of religions which is by far the largest, but has least content. I do not now take into account the dim origins, nor even those anticipations of pre-animistic conceptions which are visible among races lowest in the scale. We see at once, however, how the general cultural development, with all that belongs to it, marks the clear, characteristic steps in the advance of religious development. Clan religion, tribal religion, racial religion, all are named from the stages of social construction. Agriculture with its settled habitation becomes of the greatest significance for religion. Several villages and areas are united in larger units. Through a very complicated process, which naturally presents a different appearance at different points but is in reality one process, the gods of a religion are by unification and exclusion fathered into a divine state, ordered according to the different areas of life. Polytheism, which arose with racial religion, is a late phenomenon in the history of religion and proves itself to be a step upward, coordinate with political and cultural development, bringing with it order and a richer religious content, greater spiritual power and security, compared with the narrower religious horizon of the tribes and separate localities.

A single observation is sufficient to reveal this. According to ancient thought the god is lord only within his own territory; only there is he at home and able to aid. When Benhadad and his Syrians were defeated by Ahab, "the servants of the king of Syria said unto him, Their god is a god of the hills; therefore they were stronger than we; but let us fight against them on the plain, and surely we shall be stronger than they" (1 Kings 20:23).

In order to gain greater and more comprehensive divine protection, it therefore becomes necessary if possible to enrich religion with more gods and thus gradually form a pantheon, if the means and the opportunity are at hand.

A modest beginning of a pantheon was made in Israel by the new and powerful dynasty which came to the throne with Omri. His son Ahab (911-889 B.C.) married a Tyrian princess. He built a splendid temple to Melkart, the Tyrian Baal, in the new residential city of Samaria itself, and provided it with a staff of prophets. He did not in the least mean to drive out Jahweh. In the names of his children the name of Jahweh appears in its shorter form. He humbled himself before Elijah, Jahweh's prophet. But for political reasons and also for religious reasons, which can easily be imagined, he adopted, in connection with an alliance and closer contact with Tyre, its national god—in keeping with the progress of all religions of antiquity. Then arose a strange, powerful figure, rough and unyielding as granite. Elijah knew that Jahweh could tolerate no one at his side. Jahweh was a deity hostile and zealous against other gods.

In Judah they went further. With an open eye for the need of the times and the ruling desire, Ahaz (741-726 B.C.) established in a room in the palace a cult of the heavenly bodies according to the Assyrian-Babylonian model. Manasseh (696-641 B.C.) moved the images into the temple. Never in the kingdom of Judah has religious zeal in conjunction with politics cultivated and adopted so many ancient Canaanitish or absolutely foreign rites as during the reign of Manasseh and of Amon (641-639 B.C.). Ezekiel tells us what he saw in the temple and beside it in Jerusalem (chap. 8). Should not the Jerusalem temple provide itself with a pantheon just as all other shrines which kept up with the progress of the age? The temple was in a way to become a polytheistic metropolitan sanctuary. When the temple at Jerusalem of this time was able to compete with the proud shrines of foreign lands in the variety of its religious apparatus, in richness of cult and in the cruel, sacrificial, and emotionally charged demands, it was considered a step forward. We must not forget that polytheism, in its own field, is a step forward in religion, even though it was a vile thing in the eyes of the prophets, the champions of genuine Mosaism. To their contemporaries these prophets seemed hopelessly callous and godless, just as the early Christians for the piety of antiquity were *atheoi,* atheists, because of the provoking simplicity and spirituality of their faith and cult. Nevertheless, when the prophets declared open warfare on the party of progress in religion, they served the cause of religion in the future.

When the religion of race and state, with its polytheism was established, the uniform movement of culture and religion did not cease. Skill in the arts and architecture created within the religions images of the gods and temples. The images grew in magnitude in Egypt and Mesopotamia, or in richness of inventive genius in design and perhaps fantastic fullness of expression in India, or in noble human form among the Greeks. For the watering of the earth and for the needs of agriculture and of commerce on the sea, observations and computations were made of the movements of the stellar bodies and of the changes of the seasons. Theology made use of these advances. Conceptions about the gods and their worship absorbed more and more of the higher ethical elements together with a parallel progress in social ethics. The more complicated and refined mode of life reacted upon religion.

Polytheism is not the last word of culture-religion. Even the divine state at times becomes strongly monarchial in order. Partly because of political reasons, as in the case of Marduk, Ashur, Amon, and Jupiter, or for other reasons, as with Zeus and Indra, one god becomes lord or ruler over the rest. Strong expression of pious zeal in the worship of divine power is found in all stages of polytheism and must not be confused with the tendency to unite the gods as forms of one single deity or as the name of the unfathomable being behind heaven and earth.

Individual approaches toward monotheism in the area of naturereligions and polytheism have never succeeded. In the reign of Rammannirari III in Assyria (811-783 B.C.) it seems that a governor of Kalah and other provinces wished to make Nabu the only god. To please the king and his mother, who probably was a Babylonian princess, he dedicated eight images to Nabu, the deity of Borsippa, Babylon's neighboring city, with inscriptions which called upon the people to put their trust in this god and in none other. In the year 807 B.C. a splendid temple was erected to Nabu in Kalah.[5]

Still more comprehensive and important is the attempt in Egypt of Huen-Aten, Amenhotep IV, during the eighteenth dynasty to break with the old religious tradition and worship the disk of the sun, Aten-Ra, alone as god. It can be questioned whether such a monotheism, in which a nature god carries the whole cult and faith, really meant progress. The undertaking was at all events doomed to failure. All that resulted was a unique episode to which the discoveries at El-Amarna, where the religion-reforming Pharaoh built himself a new capital, bear eloquent testimony. A prince in Texcuco in old Mexico, Netzalcuatl, is said to have worshiped one divinity without images and without bloody sacrifices. Something similar is related of a prince of the Incas in Peru, Tupak Yupomki. Neither succeeded in carrying out his plans of reform.

To parallel such "monotheism," depending on the will either of an enlightened or of a capricious ruler, with Jahweh-monotheism[6] is to misunderstand the clear story of the history of religion. No

---

[5] C. P. Tiele, *Geschiedenis van den Godsdienst in de Oudheid,* Vol. I (Amsterdam: P. N. van Kampen, 1893), p. 178.

[6] H. Winckler, *Abraham als Babylonier, Joseph als Ägypter: Der weltgeschichtliche Hintergrund der biblischen Vätergeschichten auf Grund der Keilinscriften dargestellt* (Leipzig: Hinrichs, 1903).

nature-god or culture-god has ever been able to achieve a real monotheism of universal or spiritual nature. For this achievement there was needed the revelation of the prophets.

In the exercise of thought the powers of speculation and abstraction are trained and logical demands are sharpened. In India there enters with the Upanishads a new period for religion in connection with a view of the phenomenality of the world. The subtlety of mind and the consistency of thought shown in the carrying of this thought into abstract idealism and acosmism is in no sense inferior to similar later operations of thought in Greece and in modern times.

Among peoples noted for intellectual acumen, chiefly those of India and Persia, this aspect of culture has brought new epochs for religion. With the spiritualizing of the conception of God followed the vanishing of the figures of the gods. The Eternal Being of Brahmanism became finally so emptied of religious content that at least one of the many teachers of salvation and organizers of orders, Gautama Buddha, did away with this figure entirely. It had become an insufferable weight, a burden to the seeker of salvation. None, I emphasize, none of the polytheistic gods, the gods which in accordance with the law of the spiritual unity of man have followed the development of culture, has in the long run been able to endure the rarefied atmosphere of the highest elevations of spiritual culture. Not one. The living divine beings have faded away or have been lost in "the Great Unknown." They have become wrapped in "the sacred twilight" or have been swallowed up in "the divine darkness."

We can trace clearly the development into polytheism, monarchic supremacy, and from thence out into pantheism, idealism, acosmism or religious agnosticism. The figures of the gods of nature-religion and culture-religion emerge out of prehistoric shadows in fantastic, shapeless animal phantoms, which then take on form, order, refinement, human qualities, and then these numerous, but not innumerable throngs march past us, well-defined forms indeed. They continue their march and are lost in the evening shadows on the horizon. Culture is doomed to fail and wither away, or commit suicide in the philosophical conclusion that labor is in vain and culture itself without meaning, unless it is borne up by a strong and vital religious faith.[7] The religion which merely accompanies this cultural development, without infusing new elements of revelation, shares its fate. Is China an exception? No, Laotse's *tao* has very little left of a living deity. In the religion of the state, the ethical reform of Confucius left a minimum of divine worship for the sake of the community. Reasons of state and reverence for authority have been stronger than the spiritual demands of culture. Pagan Rome, in its way, might have become a counterpart, had it but survived.

The second great world-historic development belongs, if we except eastern Asia, to the Semitic and the Indo-Germanic peoples. Two ancient folk gods have there been able to maintain themselves, Ahura-Mazda and Jahweh, an Aryan and a Semitic folk god. But this has been possible just because and only because something other than cultural religion, something new, has there emerged. Because of a new prophetic content these gods have escaped the fate of those of the culture-religions, even though Ahura-Mazda later tended more toward polytheism than did the Mosaic revealed religion in Israel or did the gospel still later in the church.

The dissolution of polytheism by the higher intellectual and moral culture into pantheism and idealism does not mean the destruction of all personal divine beings. For this development did not penetrate to the masses. Folk religion demands a living deity. New gods spring up. Buddhism procured itself many such Buddhas and Budhisatvas without any warrant being found for them in the writings or claims of Buddha himself. Of all sects and religions which, without contact with revealed religion, have grown up on a

[7] Cf. V. Norström, *Vad vi behöfva: En blick på samtidens vetande och tro* (Stockholm: Bonniers, 1901); *Radikalism ännu en gång* (Stockholm: Hierta, 1903). Also R. Eucken, *Der Wahrheitsgehalt der Religion* (Leipzig: Viet, 1901); trans. W. Tudor Jones, *The Truth of Religion* (New York: Putnam, 1911).

soil that had been prepared by the higher intellectual culture in India and the ancient world, two, namely, Krishnaism in India and Mithraism in the Roman world, have shown a remarkable power to make vivid the certainty of the comforting nearness and living presence of their deities in a way that has given to these a characteristic difference from the ancient national divinities. Both Krishna and Mithra are equipped with human experiences and human achievements in a way different from that with which the myths have related the story of the polytheistic gods. To them has been joined a bit of invented salvation story. That kind of Jesus worship, which is called "evangelism" (although this name hardly fits because it lacks the moral salt of the evangel and the purification of personality which constitutes the uniqueness of historical revealed religion), often reveals in its language and terms of expression a striking similarity to these and other cults from the later culture of India and the ancient world. They are so similar that the name of Krishna or of Mithra or of some other can be substituted for the name of Jesus. But monotheistic these cults are not. Their mediators cannot by any power of the imagination or by condensation of religious emotion and tradition be changed into that which no human operation, after all, can establish, a historic revelation of the divine.

Culture and religion accompany each other, as we have seen, although with disparateness and unevenness. The road leads to polytheism, and then farther on, away again from polytheism, to unity, but never to a real, monotheistic, universal faith in the living God.

The exceptions are easily counted. The more sharply do they stand out. Zoroaster's Ahura-Mazda was fundamentally monotheistic. He is not a tribal god beside others. (The daevas are combated not as gods but as devils.) He is not the highest in a pantheon of nature gods. In the Gathas he is surrounded by celestial servants, not rivals. No divine figure outside the Bible approaches him in spirituality and monotheistic exaltation. And what about the culture? The reform of Zoroaster was not only a religious but an economic reform, one of the primitive among these. It marks the transition from the life of hunting and nomadic habits to that of settled dwellings and ordered labor in field and pasture. The great cultural nations, however, have not been able to bring forth a conception of God such as Zoroaster's, even on the higher levels of civilization, when they had left this transition so far in the dim past that it had faded from memory.

Still more striking is the difference in the relation which the prophetic religion of Israel bore to general culture. The recently unified tribes, arriving as barbaric conquerors, came into contact with the Canaanite culture, which for one or more millenniums had been saturated with Babylonian civilization. This higher culture, with agriculture, vineyards, and city life, they gradually acquired. And yet, after a long period of the monarchy had elapsed, the powerful, genuine Mosaism rises again in league with nomadic life against the higher development of tilling the soil, planting vineyards, and building cities, with all the accompanying advantages. It is a pity that H. S. Vodskov never gave us the second volume of his great work on *Sjeledyrkelse og Naturdyrkelse* ("Worship of Souls and Worship of Nature"). In this book, although only a fragment, through which he made himself a never-fading name among Scandinavian scholars, he makes the following daring statement: "Man, at the higher hunting and nomadic stage is inferior to the civilized man in all material arts and achievements, but he is just as much superior to him in religion, language and social structure."[8] He gives as an example from religions, the worship of souls. This never gained the power in nomadic life which it did in the settled state. Vodskov's statement is a direct contradiction of the law of the spiritual unity of mankind. But is it true in a general application? It is true, if what one means is that *one nomadic* people attained among the religions of the world a greater importance than all agricultural peoples combined. The higher, prophetic

---

[8] [H. S. Vodshov, *Sjaeledyrkelse og naturdyrkelse:bidrag til bestemmelsen af den mytologiske metode* (Copenhagen: Lehmann & Stage, 1897), p. xliv.]

religion asserts itself even in company with a lower level of culture, yes, even in antagonism to a higher civilization. Budde points out that it was fortunate that the Rechabites, who were Mosaists inimical to civilization, did not gain the victory, for Jahweh became the giver and lord of the higher civilization as well. Thereby the older Jahwism was freed from that austerity, which is so repelling and inhuman to us. But if we ask whence that element had its origin which has been so fruitful and indispensable for the religious life of humanity, from nomadic Mosaism or from the settled life under Canaanite influence, when Jahweh acquired the characteristics of the culture gods without losing his identity, the answer cannot be uncertain. It was through Moses that the religion of Jahweh was hindered from pursuing the usual course of culture-religion. The trend toward polytheism was stopped in spite of natural tendencies and efforts, and the Jahweh religion was prevented from dissolving into pantheism and idealism. The highest spiritual and ethical conception of God in the gospel only serves to bring him closer and make him more living than ever. Perhaps it was earlier even than Moses. The Old Testament knows of no special revelation to Abraham.[9] Attempts to determine historically what is the contribution of Abraham to religion have, hitherto at least, proved unsatisfying, for the reason, among others, that they prove too much or must deal with only general and formless conceptions. This is true even of such attempts to bring to light an Abrahamic religion as resolutely take their stand on scientific grounds, as that of A. Klostermann, who attempts to vindicate in his *Geschichte des Volkes Israel* a "spiritual, personal character" for the "peculiar religion of Abraham."[10] Up to the time of Moses, religion seems not yet to have reached the crossroads, where the road to polytheism and "the divine" abstractions leads off from the way to the living God, never to meet it again. Have we the right to expect information about

[9] Cf. Rudolph Kittel, *Geschichte des Volkes Israel* (3rd ed.; Gotha: F. A. Perthes, 1916-17).
[10] August Klostermann, *Geschichte des Volkes Israel* (Munich: C. H. Beck, 1896).

Abraham in the cuneiform inscriptions, or at least such information as will permit conclusions and well-based combinations concerning the religion of Abraham? Hugo Winckler writes: "These documents are official writings and one cannot expect of them that those matters should have importance for them which the course of history has shown to be determining in the development of the world. The importance, for example, that Kant has won for the spiritual life of the modern world cannot be discovered from the state archives of his own time. Humanity has not been able within the short span of a generation to recognize the importance of the life work of its leading personalities."[11] However, the certainty with which Assyriological research has moved in the vast distances of the past—vast, and yet in comparison with the existence of the race so insignificant—has taken away something of the skeptical fear, which, without further discussion, considered it unscientific to hold the patriarchs to be what tradition with one voice proclaims them, historical personalities. Even though it be precarious to seek in the time of Abraham an epoch of radical importance for the religion of Israel—the importance for religion that Abraham later won as "the father of the faithful" is another matter—yet it is impossible to place the epoch-making element in revealed religion *after* the time of Moses. To quote J. W. Rothstein, "One must finally, with Reuss, allow it to stand, that the foundation of the religious development of the Old Testament was laid where, according to the Biblical tradition it was laid, in the time of Moses and through Moses."[12] The great prophets, an Amos, a Hosea, an Isaiah, a Jeremiah, the psalmist Ebed-Jahweh, the author of the Psalm 73, sometimes reveal in religious faith and morals an elevation which even the twentieth Christian century has not been able to attain. The distance between them and the most beautiful examples of Babylonian documents quoted by Delitzsch is as the

[11] Winckler, *op. cit.*, p. 24.
[12] J. W. Rothstein, *Der Gottesglaube im alten Israel und die religionsgeschichtliche Kritik* (Halle: Müller, 1900), p. 45. Cf. also the works of E. Stave and S. A. Fries.

distance between heaven and earth.[13] They move on a different, a higher plane. It is self-evident, it verges almost upon a truism, to note the fact that in the degree in which the prophetic faith of Israel rises above the religion of Babylon, by just so much does the general culture of Babylon, the spiritual capital, the *ville lumière* of its day, with its science, its art, its social development, and its ancient history, rise above Israel, that queer upstart on the banks of the Jordan. The redemption of the world, the unconquerable certainty of faith in the loving will of the living God based on Jesus Christ, after all has not come from Babylon, or Athens, or Rome, but from Galilee and Jerusalem.

Of course, it is possible to find the prophetic religion in the guise of a culture-religion, accompanied by the higher humanities and intellectual life of the times. To find this, one must go to the Hellenistic Judaism of the Diaspora and to Christianity, when it had robed itself in the rich spiritual garments of antiquity. But if this dazzling sight deceives us and produces the illusion that the secret of the triumphant advance of Christianity was Greek philosophy, art, science and social power, history abundantly proves that the power and the victory came rather from the gospel and the prophetic movement, poor in culture, but not hostile to culture nor deficient in culture. Jesus does not belong to the history of cultural religion. Jesus, the fulfiller of Moses and the prophets, did not come to establish a new religion, but rather to do away with all religions and establish the kingdom of God. A religion with all the characteristics of such has risen out of his legacy. But this is only a transition, a means toward the end, the kingdom of God. It is not yet made manifest what we shall be.

The religion of the prophets is not a stage in the development of religion, but a phenomenon by itself. Attempts to make it the product of the development of national religion, fascinating as they may be, are contrary to the actual records of the history of religions.

[13] H. Gunkel, *Israel und Babylonien* (Göttingen: Vandenhoeck & Ruprecht, 1903), pp. 37 f. [trans. "E.S.B.," *Israel and Babylon: The Influence of Babylon on the Religion of Israel* (Philadelphia: J. J. McVey, 1904).]

The influence of great personalities on religion we note in many places. They concentrate in the period from the eighth to the sixth centuries before Christ, in widely separated lands: Laotse, Confucius, Zoroaster, Buddha, the literary prophets of Israel, and the earlier Greek teachers of redemptive religion. But did these come with new creative religious ideas? Did they speak in the name of the living God? Confucius was an ethical and social teacher. Laotse had a more speculative and inward quality. But we have already had cause to ask if in his faith there is found any love of a living and active deity. Gautama Buddha released religious blessedness and the way to it from the very idea of God. In Greece not one of the great personalities of the higher and nobler piety was able to express his experience of God in a prophetic proclamation of the rule and living power of God, even though the faith of some, especially of the later Stoics, due to the experience of Socrates, has much of the temper of prophetism. The last and finest religious creation of the Greek spirit, Neoplatonism, the chief exponent of which, Plotinus, is considered by Augustine to be the best interpreter of Plato, has all the characteristics of polytheism refined into pantheism and idealism, and of spiritualized and ethicized mysticism. With its contemplation and ecstatic union with the "Unspeakable" as the ideal form of piety, this mysticism is both a nature mysticism and a mysticism of infinity in contrast to the personal mysticism of the prophetic movement.

There remain the work of Zoroaster and of Moses and the prophets. The religion of Zoroaster, however, does not count in the main for the history of religion, owing to its own narrow limitations and to the fact that it was never fully carried out. There is something appealing in the thought that the Jewish piety in contact with the Persian religion recognized in it something of its own religious faith and was therefore sensitive to influence from it. The voice of God spoke of Cyrus through the mouth of the prophet: "Behold my servant, whom I have chosen" (Isa. 45). But it is clear that Cyrus did not have the reformed Mazda faith. The reli-

gious experience and revelation of God which has been most penetrating and significant for the religious history of mankind, the prophetic religion, arises in a very humble cultural surrounding, separated from the stream of the great, widespread development of
society, of ethics, of culture and thought. Culture has since adopted
it, from it received a new soul, and has been saved from self-destruction. Although culture has in turn influenced this religion, it
has not given to it any new religious power.

This does not mean that the prophets came into history, detached
from that which preceded them, outside the cultural continuity. No
prophet, no revelation, ever comes before the fullness of time, or
until the necessary conditions are at hand (Mark 1:15; Gal. 4:4).
These conditions are of historical and psychological nature. They
are such that they exclude entirely the conception of divine arbi-
trariness. No hiatus, no leap takes place. The psychological and historical continuity is unbroken. And yet, the religion of the prophets
offers for the science of religion a different and a much more
difficult problem than that of nature-religion or culture-religion. It
is not solved by simply saying, we do not see the continuity, therefore it must be God's work. This would be a theological subterfuge,
as dangerous as it is comfortable, thus to put God in where the continuity is not clear. This is the mode of thought upon which Posi-
tivism proceeds when it holds that God is the explanation of all the
unknown, and, in the measure that enlightenment spreads its illumination, there is less need of God as an explanation. Not so. The
divine is revealed in the human. We cannot discover any gap in the
historical and psychological continuity of the life of the prophet.
Had we the eyes of God all would lie clearly before us in its continuous process. Neither can we in the prophetic religion draw a
line around certain words or certain events and say, here is God and
revelation, there is man and nature. Even in the perfect revelation
of God in the person of Christ the divine and the human are com-
mingled, as the theologians have expressed in the doctrine of the
communicatio idiomatum.

It is not our ignorance nor the obscurity of the problem which mark the divine in the work of the prophets. It is not the difficulty and darkness which surround the origin of the prophetic religion which is the determining element. Rather, it is the clear insight that a new stream of profound religious content, which itself points to an immediate contact with God as its source, has come into the world through the prophets. "Every genius on earth is a puzzle for history. The greatest genius is always the religious genius. Every new creation of genius can be only partially explained by the times. There is always left a remainder, something inexplicable. The greatest remainder of this sort is always left by the creative religious genius, by him who lays hold more deeply upon the mysterious basis of life."[14] In the prophetic religion there breaks forth a living stream of immediate experience of the divine more powerful than ever appears in culture-religion. This implies, as we shall see, a knowledge of God which is richer than, and in an essential way different from, that which is outside of the prophetic religion. We have already seen that it comes forth in a unique way in the history of religion, in a relative independence of the course of general culture, which discredits completely the law of the spiritual unity of the race, conceived in the manner above pointed out. Far better it would be to postulate for this law in the spiritual history of humanity a law of the distribution of tasks. This gives the task of culture to some peoples, for example, the Babylonians. Their significance for the history of religion would have been lost in the sands if it had not been for the fact that the prophetic religion of Israel had taken up and reshaped some elements of the ancient wisdom of this highly cultured people. This law has chosen out one people to be pre-eminently the people of religion and to build for the future of religion.

"The analogy of members in a body, by which the apostle Paul, in a manner unsurpassed, describes the relation in which every indi-

[14] R. Kittel, *Der Babel-Bibel-Streit und die Offenbarungsfrage* (Leipzig: Deichert, 1903), p. 12. Cf. also his *Gestalten und Gedanken in Israel* (Leipzig: Quelle & Meyer, 1925).

vidual in a community, with his special vocation and his own talents and gifts, stands to the community itself in its entirety, can be applied also to nations in respect to their role and their significance for the great family of humanity. And as the life of the body most intimately depends on the proper function of small organs, the heart, the brain, the lungs, etc., so nations may have a function which does not depend on their size, their military strength or even upon their culture and refinement."[15] Since the metaphysical and metahistorical venture of faith has been made from the awareness and certainty of the divine to the conception of God, his creation, his self-impartation, his revelation, it is difficult for one to avoid clearly distinguishing in the history of religion a unique revelation, that of the prophetic religion, the revealed religion, in the course of sacred history throughout the ages.

But is not the conception of a unique revelation, of a chosen people of religion, an unworthy one and contrary to the love and justice of God? This ancient objection of Celsus has weight even today. According to him Jews and Christians believed that God had for their sake established the earth and the heavens. He compares the Christians to worms, and pictures them as coming forth and saying: "The heavens God sets aside, and the earth, great as it is, he forsakes, to employ himself only with us and to have relations with us alone. To us he sends messengers constantly and seeks to unite us with himself eternally" (Origen, *Contra Celsum IV.* 27, 28.). I pass by Origen's confutation of Celsus with the Scriptural statements of the all-embracing power and love of God and the universality of redemption. But it is one thing to reckon what God *ought* to have done according to our ideas of him and his being. It is another thing to investigate so far as is possible for us what he actually *has done* in the life and history of mankind. I see very clearly how much more fascinating for apologetics is that view of Christianity, which holds that it is the flower of the development of religion, its final end, into which all the different lines of general revelation have converged.

[15] N. Ignell, *Menskliga utvecklingens historia,* Vol. II (Stockholm, 1862), p. 345.

In the world of thought, in a transcendent view of evolution,[16] Christianity can of course be designated as the highest stage of development or its end, as the point where a new species has been formed, where a new life, that of the superman, the superhuman life (as we Christians say, the divine-human life) has appeared. Apologetics has the full right to claim that in Christianity we have a higher unity, above the absorption of Zoroastrianism in culture, above Buddhism's denial of culture, above the theocracy of Semitic religion and the theanthropy of the Arians, above the divine immanence and transcendence. But historically something else has happened. The land of Israel was so situated that the prophetic religion came into contact with other religions and other civilizations. Through this it received incalculable material and impulse for the perfecting and the determining of its own unique character through the reshaping or else the rejection of this foreign element. Abraham came from Mesopotamia, Joseph and Moses came from Egypt. In this, according to Winckler, there lies before us in general contours the history of a whole culture.[17] In Canaan Israel came daily in contact with the native religions. For a century it has been held as certain that belief in resurrection and in a devil came from the Parsees. Certain it is that the Jews learned to know Mazda worship. Later Judaism shows the influence of Hellenism. The rich and significant work of W. Bousset, *Die Religion des Judentums im neutestamentlichen Zeitalter*,[18] has a sixth and final section with the title, "The Problem of the History of Religion," which is summarized as follows: "The progressively unified life of humanity and its religious development drew Judaism more and more powerfully into its stream." "Authenticated influences penetrate into the very center of its religion." "Not alone a *single* religion has contributed to the origin of Christianity, but contact with the whole of Western civilization, the religions of the Hellenistic period of culture."

---

[16] [What seems to be intended here is the evolutionary view that one step "transcends" the preceding one, rather than any particular evolutionary theory.]
[17] Winckler, *op. cit.*
[18] Berlin: Reuther & Reichard, 1903.

"Judaism was the crucible into which the different elements were gathered." Such a view in general is not new. It has arisen at different times with different degrees of power, ever since the ancient Christian historical writers attempted to interpret all preceding religions as merely preparations for their own. Bousset has presented this view with scientific authority and consequent balance. But however highly these influences may be valued it is impossible to make of Christianity the *quinta essentia* of all these elements, the peak of the development of religion. In the eighteenth century, as also in our day, a number of books have been published which have found the source of the religion of Moses in the mysteries of the Egyptian priests or in some cryptic Chaldean wisdom. Now we are able to see more clearly what Israel really did receive from the East. Moses cannot be set in the line of Mesopotamian religions. We know too much for this. We realize that the most valuable element is the *exclusive property of prophetic religion*. Christianity lies before us, not as the end of the journey of religion aided by culture, but *as the full completion of a special revelation of God.*

If we wish to find an openhearted readiness to absorb everything good and true, one must turn elsewhere than to the prophets and the gospel, which are nevertheless the gold-producing vein of religion in the world. The ideal of humanity in Hellenism also contained religious elements of significant nature, which came most clearly to light in the immortally beautiful swan song of the Hellenic spirit, Neoplatonism. On its scale every tone of the whole religious development of humanity readily found a place—all except Judaism and Christianity, because of their unreasonable demands. Plotinus (d. A.D. 270) would not even mention the land of his birth, according to his biographer, Porphyrios. The biographer of Proclus (d. A.D. 485) tells us that he considered "that it was improper for a philosopher to observe the festive rites of this or that city or state, for he was to be rather the high-priest of the whole world." In the flower of Indian culture we find equally beautiful words of religious tolerance. Krishna says in *Bhagavadgita,* chapter 9, the Song of Songs of Hindu piety, that if one has a true faith and devotion to other gods, it is faith and devotion to Krishna, although in a wrong way. One is reminded of the words of Luther in *The Large Catechism,* "Only the faith and truth of the heart make either God or idol. If your faith and trust are right and sincere, you have the true God, and conversely, if your faith and trust are false and wrong, you have not the true God; for these two, God and faith, belong together and must be joined."[19]

The prophets and the Gospel speak a different language. "No one knoweth the Father except the Son and he to whomsoever the Son willeth to reveal him."[20] So far it is true, that "Christianity was in the fullest sense particularistic and rejected all other religions, while Hellenism, in the best sense of the word universalistic, awarded a certain legitimacy to every form of religion."[21] Christianity felt that it had something its own and this particularism has proved to be the strongest religious power in all the world. For in Christ it possesses that on which, in the death struggle of the human spirit, everything finally depends, certainty of the living God.

If we view the history of religion, not as progressing in accordance with our scheme of thought, but from the point of view of what it actually is, we cannot deny the fact that the interpretation given by the *Auctor ad Theophilum* of the words of Barnabas and Paul, "God suffered all the nations to walk in their own ways, and yet he left himself not without witness," is more realistic and striking than later constructions. Certainly the admonition: "Turn to the living God," marks the difference between revealed or prophetic religion and other religions of a high type. Sir Alfred C. Lyall in *Asiatic Studies* closes a review of the religious situation in

[19] [The quotation is from Luther's explanation of the First Commandment in the *Large Catechism,* in T. G. Tappert (ed.), *The Book of Concord* (Philadelphia: Muhlenberg, 1959), p. 365.]

[20] [Luke 10:22.]

[21] K. H. E. de Jong, "Plutarchus en het antieke Christendom," *Theologisch Tijdschrift,* XXXVII (1903), 315-46.

India with the statement that he is certainly not able to trace the course which imagination and thought have pursued in the progress from belief in millions of gods to the acknowledgment of an all-embracing Spirit and to the insight that he is unknowable. "I can say only, that after long personal observation of religion in India, I have received the impression that the whole marvellous construction has come through what, for want of a better expression, I must call a natural growth."[22]

III

The special relation in which this revealed religion stands to the general development of culture is matched by the inner character it possesses, which, in comparison with any corresponding religions, marks it as superior not only in degree, but essentially differing from them in those qualities which are common to all religions.

This is shown in the conception of God and of the relation to God. In what follows I am not seeking to make an evaluation, a weighing of higher and lower, but rather I shall seek to show in the most important essentials the vital difference between what I here summarize, *with the restrictions noted above,* under the designations culture-religion and revealed religion. Then, in the final analysis, it will depend upon our own personal attitude in religion to which one we shall award the precedence in its highest and purest expression.

The faith of this revealed religion is directed to *the one, living, spiritual God, who is active in history and there revealed.*

The conception of the unity of God and of his living personality in reality at once excludes the experiences and thoughts of the divine found outside the prophetic religion. Even though other religions may have a conception of God as living and active, comforting and helping, warning and punishing, in other words, a con-

[22] Sir Alfred Lyall, *Asiatic Studies, Religious and Social,* 2nd series (London: J. Murray, 1899).

ception of God that is filled with religious content, still the deity is not monotheistically conceived in religions outside of the prophetic religion. These are either at such a low stage of tribal religion, or still lower, that there can be no question of monotheism, nor even of polytheism, or else they are at the stage of polytheism, which in the history of religion shows possibilities of some development, but according to the general testimony of facts is exceedingly limited. If a striving toward unity in the conception of God has begun to assert itself, the power to retain step by step the certainty of the living, active love and power of God which awakens trust and fear, is paralyzed. At first the divine monarch is elevated above every immediate contact with the world of men, and the chain of intermediary powers is lengthened more and more. Then, on a higher plane of development, the deity disappears into the distant unknown, beyond every positive attribute. Viewed from the standpoint of religion it is perfectly consistent and really a stroke of genius that Gautama Buddha, when the sublimation had proceeded thus far, realized, with his experience and insight, that such a conception of God is without any value for the satisfaction of human longing for redemption from suffering, and made the purified religious attitude itself, Nirvana, the highest and only end of religion. It is the despairing consequence of nature-religion and culture-religion, which however proved liberating and fructifying for religion.

To be complete we should make an addition. Within the religion of India there arose, as nearly as we can determine, in the second or third century before Christ a new doctrine of redemption which differs radically from the cultivated mysticism[23] and the mysticism of infinity, which had developed either into absorption into the impersonal Brahma or else into the original methodical self-redemption of Buddhism. I mean the doctrine of Bhakti. In the *Bhagavadgita*, its classical source, in the *Bhaktisutras*, and in innu-

---

[23] [Söderblom used the term *övningsmystik* to designate the rigid inner discipline which some mystics have imposed on themselves, and contrasts it with the "mysticism of spontaneity." The "exercises" of Ignatius Loyola illustrate his meaning and suggested the term, since *övning* means "exercise" or "practice."]

merable later works, is described how salvation is won, not by human effort, but through Bhakti, "devotion," love for a personal deity. We here are concerned not with a historical revelation in a strict sense. This Bhakti redemption has never led to a real monotheism, even though in the moment of communion with the deity, the loving and worshiping soul deals with a single deity conceived as personal. Nevertheless, outside of the boundaries of the prophetic religions and of the Christian church there is no phenomenon, no doctrine of redemption, which in importance approaches the religion of Bhakti. However, we cannot in this connection do more than make the above suggestions.

What saved the conception of God from fading out of the religion of Jahweh and of the Mazda faith? As far as we can ascertain this was due, not to something which emerged in the development, such as a better ethic, a finer spirituality, individualism, or universalism, but rather it was due to the nature of the origin of these national religions. It lay in the very fact that they were *founded* religions, i.e., had personal founders.

Whatever may have been the previous history of the Ahura-Mazda religion, it is certain that before it became the religion of the chief Vistaspa and his people, as he appears in the Gathas, and finally the religion of the Persian power, it was the personal religion of Zoroaster. It had gone through the filtration of personal experience and conviction, of a prophetic consciousness of God. His experience of God brought about a radical upheaval, the importance of which can be appreciated only at a distance. Mazda became, not only as did Varuna, the highest of the gods and the guardian of the lawbound order of things *(ăsa, rta),* but in principle the only God. The other gods were excluded and became evil powers whose worship was forbidden, and his prophet knew that God, through the upheavals of history, would bring about the triumph of his cause, the cause of faith.

Within the higher religious stratum of the Greek civilization there existed a clear consciousness that the religion of Zoroaster possessed something in the direction of a vital knowledge of God, which the Greeks lacked, in spite of all their varieties of religion and their treasures of culture and their sublime philosophical power and refinement. The rhetorician Dion Chrysostom, of the first and second decade after Christ, is a high example of the monotheistic faith, as true as one could find at the time among the cultured people of the cities. Dion speaks of God as "the wisest and most worthy guide and legislator" and points out that the poets had really called "the chief and greatest god the father and king of all reasonable beings." But when there is question of the government and activity of God, of the "chariot of Zeus," Dion has a sentence to which I would call attention. "But the chariot of the mighty and holy Zeus not one of the poets has worthily celebrated in song, neither Homer nor Hesiod, but on the contrary Zoroaster and the Magi, who have learned of him." There is a feeling that Zoroaster had experienced and understood more of the being of God than the poets and wise men of Hellas.

Among the Jews two corresponding elements appear in the work of Moses with greater potency and a richer and more profound historical vitality, the idea of personality in the conception of God, and the conception of God as the God of history. How Jahweh previously had been known and worshiped is veiled in uncertainty. Will this uncertainty ever be removed? But there is scarcely room for any hesitation in believing that the experience of Moses, the revelation to Moses and through him, was the fundamental thing in the whole future history of the prophetic knowledge and worship of God in its deep differentiation from anything which was developed in the environing religions. "Through Moses Jahweh was raised above mere Nature in that he became the covenant God for seven tribes, after he had become for Moses—and here is the most important thing—the God of his life, his rescuer and helper. All of the rich future development of Jahwism above the related religions, from which in the beginning, at least in an outward way, it did not differ, has its origin in the person of Moses."[24]

[24] C. P. Tiele, *op. cit.,* I, 282 f.

In the first place, Jahweh had, through a divine self-revelation, become *the God of Moses* in a special sense before he became the God of the covenant he established.[25] In the second place, the power and love of Jahweh became known and certified by the redemption out of Egypt. Israel always remembered and never tired of celebrating the mighty deliverance of God, the extraordinary event in nature which forever bound up the new Mosaic knowledge of God in its evidence and origin with the exodus from Egypt. Most wonderful of all, a fact the significance and wide-reaching effect of which can scarcely be overestimated, was that Moses saw the *work of God in history.* The Babylonian religion also knew of a divine struggle against the violence of the sea, the battle of Marduk against the sea monster Tiamat before he killed the primeval beast and made the world out of its carcass. Gunkel has shown[26] that the Babylonian primitive tradition here and there in the Old Testament raises its head out of the popular beliefs into the literature, where otherwise the prophetic reshaping of the creation story dominates. At times the mythical struggle of the gods with the sea monster and the deliverance out of Egypt through the Red Sea are mingled indistinctly in the texts. These all are characteristic expressions of the difference between nature-religions and culture-religions, on the one hand, and the prophetic religion on the other. In nature-religions there is pictured the struggle of the deity against the wild violence of nature, of culture against nature, of order in nature against violence in nature. In the prophetic religion we have related the experience of divine will and purpose in history, the intervention of God at the significant birth of the people as a nation.

Religion has thus received a double foundation of a new kind. God is active in history, not merely in nature and the social order. God is revealed also as the living God in the consciousness of the

[25] This is the meaning of the brilliant distinction which Budde makes, which, however, hardly can be sustained, between the religion which is inherited and the Jahweism of Moses, which was a chosen religion.
[26] H. Gunkel, *Schöpfung und Chaos in Urzeit und Endzeit* (Göttingen: Vandenhoeck & Ruprecht, 1895; 2nd, ed., 1921) pp. 29 ff.

prophet, not simply sensed as the source of mysterious, infinite power in an ecstatic trance.

The differences between the work of Zoroaster and that of Moses, fraught with such great consequences for the future, come to light in the very beginning in the contrasts noted above. The activity of God in history received a powerful and gripping expression for all time in the Jewish faith in God. To this day the deliverance out of Egypt, celebrated in the Psalms, has an important place in the Jewish prayer books. The founder, the prophet, was succeeded by a line of followers through which new streams of constantly enriching impartation and knowledge of God flowed in, so that the history of the religion of Israel became, not simply a development of the content given in its beginning, but a successive re-creation, culminating and completed in Jesus Christ. There is considerable truth in the well-known saying that, strictly speaking, a religion never becomes anything more than what it was in the beginning. Its history is nothing but a spinning out, a development, a utilization of that which was given in it from the start. This is essentially true of the Mazda religion. But in Israel a new content of revelation comes in through new revealers.

The prophetic religion of Israel has especially seen the faithfulness, grace, and power of God revealed in the deliverance out of Egypt and in the personalities of the men of God, whom he has sent his people. "Also I brought you up out of the land of Egypt, and led you forty years in the wilderness, to possess the land of the Amorite. And I raised up of your sons for prophets, and of your young men for Nazarites. Is it not even thus, O ye children of Israel? saith the Lord."[27] The line of bearers and interpreters of the personal and historical divine revelation is unified into a sacred history in which the love and righteousness of the living God is delineated for faith, so that the deity can be called in a proper sense a *revealed God*, not "an unknown God," nor a hidden God. In this

[27] Amos 2:10 f. Cf. Hosea 12:13; Jer. 7:13; Deut. 18:15 ff., and other passages. J. Köberle, *Babylonische Kultur und biblische Religion* (Munich: Beck, 1903), p. 18.

sense a historical revelation is possessed by the religion of the Hebrew prophets along with and by its heir, Christianity, which sees in Jesus Christ the fulfillment of revelation, "the fullness of the godhead bodily."[28] Therefore it may be called, from the point of view of the history of religions, revealed religion in a special sense. Luther wrote in *De servo arbitrio*:

> Let God in his majesty and being alone. For as such we cannot have anything to do with him, nor has he wished that we have anything to do with him as such. But only in the measure that he is clothed and revealed in his word, by which he presents himself to us do we have anything to do with him. For the Word is his beauty and glory. The Psalmist praises him as he is clad in the Word.[29]

In bringing out this distinction I employ the *historical* point of view, not the *dogmatic*. The latter, much more important for theology, must take for its point of departure the experience which the church and the individual have of the historical redemption fulfilled in Christ, as a genuine revelation of God. Neither do I here propose the *apologetical* point of view, which makes comparisons and seeks to show the superiority of Christianity. Rather I ask: Are we justified historically in calling the biblical development of religion revealed religion in a specific sense?

The conception which the prophetic religion has of the work of God in history is revealed in the fact that the religions of Zoroaster and of Moses are the only ones which have developed a complete eschatology, with resurrection, world judgment with world restoration and perfection, and faith in a moral and religious purpose in the course of world history.[30] Not the proudest nations, not the

---

[28] [Col. 2:9.]

[29] Erlangen edition, *Opera Latina, varii argumenti* 7, 222 [Weimar edition 18, 685. *The Bondage of the Will*, trans. J. I. Packer and O. R. Johnston (London: James Clarke, 1957), p. 170. Söderblom also included the Latin original of this quotation.]

[30] Cf. my book *La vie future d'après le mazdeisme a la lumiere des croyances paralleles dans les autres religions* ("Annales du Musee Guimet Bibl. d'etudes," Part IX (Paris: Angers, 1901), chap. 4.

most ancient and excellent historical writings, not the keenest speculation outside the prophetic religions, have been able to give birth to such a profound conception of the rule of God in the world. This rule of God is sometimes realized gradually, step by step, sometimes at one swift stroke; it is a conception of divine judgment upon nations and generations, with the conception of the final perfection of the world in a perfect age. Not Rameses, not Hammurabi, not Assurbanipal, not Alexander the Great, not Caesar, have possessed the power to give such an eschatological horizon to their undertakings. "For the Greeks, as well as for their Latin disciples, the thought of meaning in the eternal struggle, of an end above the victories or defeats of the combatants, is totally wanting" (Harald Hjärne).[31] Apocalyptic and history, on the whole had no value for mysticism nor for rationalism. God's work is viewed by mysticism as timeless. Augustine, Bousset, and Hegel have sought to interpret the underlying connection of history, its meaning and its end. But they have not this conception. The philosophy of history has seen the light of day in the despised and misunderstood Jewish apocalyptic and its Parsee equivalent. "Give a man a true apocalyptic and he will be invincible," someone has said. The unconquerable confidence that the Lord has the times and the nations in his hand and that he will fulfill his faithful plans of redemption through judgment, the faith which sees purpose and reason in the course of the world in whatever form this faith has clothed itself, the invincible power in such a faith has come from the prophetic experience of God.[32]

In the prophetic conception of God lies the explanation of the peculiar fact that only the worshipers of Mazda and believers in

[31] [Harald Hjärne (1848-1922) is regarded by many as Sweden's leading historian of all time. He is credited with special skill in interpreting significant historical movements in new ways, and is regarded as a pioneer in a number of fields. His researches covered broad fields and resulted in monographs rather than in monumental volumes. These monographs and essays were collected and issued in book form, such as *Svenskt och främmande* (Stockholm, 1908). He was an associate and close friend of Söderblom at Uppsala.]

[32] Harald Hjärne, *Historiska världsbilder, in Norden* (1902), pp. 48 f. Reprinted in *Svenskt och främmande*.

Jahweh have formed a genuinely religious doctrine of the last things. This is due, not to any proximity or contact, which would make possible reciprocal influence. Other peoples have had a longer period of contact with the Persians, but have not absorbed their eschatology. Neither can it be explained as having been brought about by trying conditions or political oppression which served to compress and harden its natural elasticity and vitality for this life into a hope for the future which was to compensate for the sufferings of the present time. Other nations had been threatened and subdued by the Babylonian and Assyrian powers and by other hard taskmasters; in particular had the near blood relatives and neighbors of Israel, Amon, Moab, Edom, and whatever may be their names, suffered this fate, but have they written apocalypses and proclaimed the judgment of the world?

IV

History is the true workshop of God. So also is nature in its way. "Moses did not withdraw Jahweh from nature, quite the reverse, Jahweh rules over nature and reveals himself in it."[33] The religious experience of the prophets, however, rescued the prophetic religion from being caught in *the fatal contradiction of the nature-religions, the contradiction between nature and spirit*. For religion inevitably there comes a time when the naive confidence in the deities is shaken and the natural love of life is spent. Then begins a period of anguish of the soul. The nature deities have no answer for the deeper needs of salvation. Nature itself and the whole material phenomenal existence is dissolved by the loftier moral attitude and intellectual culture into mere appearance, a deceptive illusion, as in India, or is made something impure and evil, as in Greece. The longing for redemption finds no place of rest within the nature-religions but hurries out beyond the veil into the great unknown, to

[33] C. P. Tiele, *op. cit.*, I, 282.

the pure and timeless life of the spirit, the purity of which is conditioned by the radical negation of all that lies within the sphere of earthly existence. The contradiction between the divine and the earthly, between good and evil, blessedness and pain, purity and impurity, is identified with the contrast between the spiritual and the material. This identification reproduces the tragic and heart-rending drama of the perfected nature-religions, as we see it presented in Brahmanism and Buddhism. It is seen also in the Greek redemptive religions even before Plato. Its best known and purest types, however, are Platonism and Neoplatonism. Both in Plato and Plotinus the thoughts of the beauty of the world and its harmony run parallel. "In Plato dwell the humanist and the mystic as well." The two ideas and interests balance each other and are interwoven one with the other, and have, in their different connections, an interesting and complicated history. But the dualism is never overcome. The inner religious experience, which is fundamental in the nature-religions and culture-religions as well, is such that it knows of no point of rest in the personal, moral, and historical life, which would give it a firm foothold and a base of activity in the stream of existence. It flees instead for refuge to the dim, timeless shore of the stream across which no human eye can pierce. No light of a life-giving sun shines over the terrain of existence. The eye cannot pierce the awesome twilight, which darkens into a starless night. Religion still reveals its wonderful powers in spite of this. But when knowledge of God and experience of blessedness are weighted down with the conception of an essential dualism between spirit and body, between rest and activity, and is sought beyond all positive qualities, the result is that the bridge is destroyed between religion, on the one side, and all activity for positive ends in the world, the ethical life, and culture, on the other. Culture becomes either a farce or an enemy. Morality becomes negative. This view, if consistent, must hold that blessedness requires the stifling of the physical life or its complete abandonment. Every impulse of life must be stilled and dulled into insensibility. "Plotinus, the philosopher of our age,"—Porphyrios thus begins his biography of the master—"seems to feel ashamed that his soul dwells in a body." The attitude toward life and piety becomes essentially ascetic. Metaphysical dualism is accompanied by flight from the world in violent self-torture or else impassivity, and sets up as the religious ideal the pure enjoyment of contemplation and ecstasy (as in ecstatic mysticism) or of unbroken tranquillity (as in quietistic mysticism). However high a place morality may reach on the Jacob's ladder which leads to blessedness, it always remains only a means of purification, a way to attain, and never becomes distinctly a service of God.

The prophetic religions of Israel and Iran prove themselves to be the only ones which have broken through this barrier of a contradiction between spirit and body, and have thereby cut the roots of the ascetic ideal of life. This is due to the basic experience of God as redemptive, ethical, loving will. He is too exalted to tolerate any image-making and worship under any outward form. The images of the deities of the advanced Babylonian culture, as well as the images and fetishes of Canaan, were judged by the genuine Mosaism, not as they truly are in the history of polytheism, as an advance together with culture, but as abominations. Neither the images of Jahweh as a bull nor the image of Ahura-Mazda which was worshiped by the great king according to the manner of Mesopotamian art as shown in the inscription of Darius at Behistun constitute any real exception to the enmity which the genuine religions of Moses and Zoroaster always showed against images of the deity, an enmity which was astounding to the ancient world and without parallel in the history of religions. Herodotus is surprised that "the Persians do not raise any statues, temples or altars, but even consider it folly to do so, for they do not consider, as do the Greeks, that the gods have any human form" (I, 131). The development in the prophetic religion, however, is something entirely different from that which takes place at the higher stage of nature-religion, when the divine is conceived of as the abstract unity beyond the multiplicity, as the pure being only negatively to be defined, to make images of which would be absurd and a return to the naive stage. Here the standpoint of culture is something different. The lack of images in the prophetic religion does not mean that the divine becomes something ethereal and distant, indefinable. Quite the contrary. For the prophetic religion an image means a dead thing (Isa. 44), but the Lord is living and active. The image is a created thing, the Lord is the Creator. Tht contrast is not that of spirit versus bodily form, but rather that of Creator above the created, the living, jealous God above every image or likeness. The same observation can be made in reference to the sacrificial cult. In India, long before Buddha, as also in Greece, this was abandoned on the higher stage, as as baser, concrete form, which the spiritual conception did not need, or as a worship which no longer gave comfort to the heart in its longing for redemption. Who does not see that here too the burning, passionate polemic of the prophets in the name of God himself is of a different order? God does not need sacrifice; he does not want sacrifice, but justice and righteousness.

Does a *monistic* conception belong then to the essence of the prophetic religion? No. In the prophetic religion there emerges another dualism, which is not a metaphysical, speculative one, a contrast between spirit and matter, but a practical, moral, and religious dualism. It is not revealed from the beginning. The daevas against which Zoroaster fought in the name of Ahura-Mazda, were viewed as evil spirits, which was not the case with the Baals, against which Mosaism fought in the name of Jahweh. Even the Gathas know a devil, *druj,* "The Lie" *par préférence,* the antagonist, "the evil Spirit," as the name of this power of untruth and death is formulated. He is not a nature deity, nor the material and sensual world, which we know from the Gnostic systems, but the spiritual principle and lord of evil and selfish prudence. The two spirits, between which choice must be made in the battle of life, were found (according to Yasna 30) in the beginning and created first of all—life and death, heaven for the good and hell for the wicked. In the

Gathas death only is the territory of "the Evil One." The Lord has created all, light and darkness,[34] sleep and wakefulness, morning, noon and night (Yasna 44). Afterwards all of creation was divided between the two. According to the later view, Anra Mainya created the evil powers, unclean beasts, evil celestial bodies, etc., over against the pure creations of the Lord. But this dualism is never confused with the contrast: spirit versus body. The latter is also named constantly in the *Avesta*. But the devil has his following in the spiritual as well as the physical world. The Lord gave the fravashis, the fylgias, a body with which to fight against evil. His are the pure elements, earth, fire, water. This dualism does not hinder the Mazda religion from being a religion most directly friendly to culture, the most anti-ascetic and optimistic religion that ever existed.[35]

Why did not Zoroaster rather than Buddha become the light of Asia? Why did not the vigorous champion of useful work, of the power of life, purity, and health in the rewarding service of the Lord win the hearts of men, instead of the gentle, sympathetic interpreter of the pain of the world and of Nirvana, the stillness of death? I am not capable of giving the full answer to this complex question, which is bound up with the difference between India and Iran and a series of related historical events. One sentence in the answer must at all events be the following: Zoroaster had not sufficiently sounded the depths of suffering.[36] The power of a religion is not to be judged by its hymns of praise, but by its experience of the misery and darkness of life. Only *one* religion has gone as far down into the abyss as the religion of the pain of the world, the Indian religion, yes, deeper than the Indian religion. This religion is Christianity. But the message of salvation in the former becomes pessimistic; the true life is the stillness of death. In the lat-

[34] Cf. Isa. 45:7.
[35] See my "Du Genie du Mazdéisme," in *Mélanges de Harlez* (Leiden, 1896), pp. 298-302.
[36] *La vie future,* p. 392. Cf. the presentation of the problem of life and death which I have given in this work, chap. 5.

ter it becomes optimistic in spite of the infernal depths, an eternal Yea against all Nay, as Carlyle said in briefest form, or in the apostle's words as these are given in II Corinthians 1:20: "All the promises of God are yea in Jesus Christ." The revealed religion, perfected in Christianity, is not caught in the metaphysical dualism, but has broken through it by its experience of the will of God through love, acting redemptively in spirit and nature.

For more than a hundred years it has been an axiom that the dualism of later Judaism and of Christianity has come from Parseeism. This is not the place to examine the truth of this opinion. It is sufficient here to say that the dualism in Judaism and Christianity (and Islam) is of the same kind with that in Parseeism, the contrast between God and the devil, between the divine, victorious will of love and radical, inexplicable evil, between life and death, confidence and despair, heaven and hell, the single combat which we wage in the world between good and evil (Eph. 6:11 ff.). It is not the metaphysical contrast between spirit and matter, unity and multiplicity, indefinable being and the world. Is not the belief in devils recorded in the Gospels as shared by the contemporaries of Jesus a black spot from the dark times on the bright picture of the joyful message of the gospel? The demand is made, that this dualism can and ought to be removed, as something which has come in from the outside and is essentially foreign and antagonistic. This perhaps is a very common view.[37] I cannot see but that the deeper experience of sin, suffering and distress, which is the strength of religion, by necessity led from the monism of the prophets to the dualism of the Gospels and that this development is one of the most significant within revealed religion. There are not lacking signs of such an insight in modern theology.[38] Jesus has sharpened

[37] Cf. W. Bousset, *Die judische Apokalyptik* (Berlin: Reuther & Reichard, 1903), pp. 61 f. Bousset adds, however: "The dualism was the covering for the tremendous ethical seriousness and religious depth of the gospel." Thereby the common rationalistic view is overcome.

[38] A. Harnack, *Die Mission und Ausbreitung des Christentums* (1st ed.; Leipzig: J. Hinrichs, 1902), pp. 92 ff. [trans. James Moffat, *The Expansion of Christianity in the First Three Centuries* (New York: G. P. Putnam's Sons, 1904-1905).]

this dualism, not weakened it. No one has penetrated farther into the problem of evil than he with the words: "An enemy hath done this."[39] Jesus presents no theodicy, no defense for God in the terrible and mysterious trial of sin and misery, defense of the kind which the friends of Job had on their tongues and about which apologetics in all ages has shown much well meaning concern. All attempts within Christianity to escape from or to get over this dualism have either weakened the power which lies in the courageous realism of the gospel, or else led to the absurdity of putting the dualism in the very being of God. This holds true also of all attempts to make of evil but a shadow in and for the harmony of the picture, an element necessary to a higher development. The latter explanation will always have to face the answer which the Hollander, Robbert Robbertsz, gave two strict Calvinist ministers when they sought to put him in a tight place with the problem of the origin of sin. "When the first sin was committed Adam put the blame on the woman and the woman put the blame on the serpent. The serpent, who was as yet young and dull, made no answer. Now he has become old and confident and comes to the synod of Dort and says that God has done it." In Jesus one seeks vainly for any theory of any sort. The theodicy of Jesus is not an interpretation for the intellect, but a task for the will: "Watch and pray." "Deliver us from evil." It is also a sure confidence of the outcome: "Now is the judgment of this world, now shall the prince of this world be cast out." "Every plant which my heavenly Father planted not, shall be rooted up."[40] But Jesus also has prevented the dualism of the religious and moral life from becoming entangled in any dualism of nature. All of life, all of existence is its scene. Decision is made in solitude as the soul meets God, who is the God of Jesus Christ and our God. Thence power is received. Afterwards the battle in the moral and cultural life is fought out with positive tasks, with real conquests for the kingdom of God. Luther knows the two

[39] [Matt. 13:28.]
[40] [Matt. 26:41; 6:13; John 12:31; Matt. 15:13.]

kinds of escape from the world. He takes seriously the words of the Gospel: "I pray not that thou shouldest take them out of the world, but that thou shouldest keep them from the evil one."[41] It is of this preservation in the midst of life's bitter struggle that Paul sings his song of victory in Romans, chapter eight: "I am persuaded." His words are the echo of those of the psalmist in the 73rd Psalm: "Lord, when I have thee" (Swedish trans.). The battle cry of religion is not: "Gilding the world," nor, "Escape from the world," but, "Overcoming the world."

V

The place of this new experience of God, which in the history of religion constitutes a unique species of revelation, was the soul life of the prophets. They heard the voice of the Eternal and saw his hand outstretched over nations and ages. What was transacted between them and God belongs to the mysteries of the inner life. But in communion with the divine in the invisible sanctuary lies the basis for the clear distinction we can see between prophetic religion and nature-religion, between revealed religion and culture-religion. The investigation of the elemental forms of this higher religious experience belongs to the great and urgent tasks of the psychology of religion. The theological psychology of religion, as exemplified by W. Herrmann, has clear insight into the essential difference, but operates with an all too limited material. Its point of view is of great value for the cultivation of religion and for the needs of the church, but leaves out of reckoning important phenomena of essential mysticism within revealed religion, in the Christian era and before Christ as well. The present day psychology of religion in France, in America and England, and in other lands as well, has not yet arrived at a decisive recognition of this difference with which we here are concerned. This is due to the fact that in the

[41] [John 17:15.]

main it has hitherto concerned itself with more general types and phenomena. In America it has gathered by the statistical method a mass of religious confessions. It has not concentrated its labor upon the great religious personalities, who have handed down to us descriptions of their own inner life. A psychology of religion which does not give its attention primarily to men like the prophets, St. Paul, Augustine, Luther, Pascal, and Kierkegaard, can no doubt make an important and promising contribution. The work of William James is an excellent proof of this. But one cannot expect that it will be able to enter into the deep problems of the psychology of personal mysticism.

May it not be that this task in scientific religious thought is assigned to Christian thinkers of Scandinavia? It is certain that in the history of our religious thought the significance of the conception and symbol of personality is older and more deeply rooted than elsewhere. In Sweden there has been for at least a century a golden thread running through all of our spiritual culture. This golden thread is that personalistic philosophy which has as its foremost and typical representative the powerful personality of Erik Gustaf Geijer.[42] Its matchless architect was the philosopher Boström.[43] Its refined and profound analyst of the inner life was Pontus Wikner.[44] Its universal spirit was Victor Rydberg.[45] The building erected by Boström was so perfect, so splendid, that for a time it seemed as though the end of all labor had come. Succeeding generations, so it seemed, desiring to live and labor must leave the perfected system in its beauty as a glorious mausoleum and seek out other sites if they would build anything new. This did not, however,

[42] [Erik Gustaf Geijer (1783-1847) was a popular Swedish poet, historian, and cultural analyst.]

[43] [Christopher J. Boström (1797-1866), professor of philosophy at Uppsala. Sweden's best known and most influential philosopher, he was a "Christian Platonist" who corrected Plato by emphasizing the conscious life and personality, as compared with abstract ideas.]

[44] [Pontus Wikner (1837-1888), a Swedish philosopher in the same general pattern as Boström; he diverged from Boström on the grounds that the latter would end in pantheism.]

[45] [Viktor Rydberg (1828-1895), Swedish writer and poet whose interests ranged widely over philosophy, literature, cultural history, and aesthetics.]

prove to be the case. Swedish thought, in moving on, has not broken its continuity in the depths. The conception of religion in all genuine preaching in Sweden, in philosophical and theological science, in devotional address, in song and literature testifies to this. In spite of differences on the surface, there is a common appreciation of the significance of personality.

The same is true of Denmark, the land of Kierkegaard and Grundtvig. "However far the thinkers have differed one from another, they have all, as one man, centered upon the principle of personality. It has not, as has continually happened in Germany, been lost sight of, not even by Broechner. At this point, even the Germanized Martensen reveals that he is Danish. This is the height we attained in Kierkegaard. This is where the lasting validity of Rasmus Nielsen[46] is found. Today every modern thinker in Germany is talking about 'Christian personality.' This language was familiar to us at a time when it was scarcely mentioned in Germany. How has not this idea penetrated all our thinking."[47] The investigation of the psychology of religious experience is foredoomed to be halted before the mystery of the personal individual life. It can, however, serve to bring a clearer light to bear upon an important contrast between two main types of religious experience. I do not here refer to that contrast which exists between an artificial and professional experience, on the one hand, and a genuine and meaningful one on the other. This latter difference is found even in the highest ecstasy of nature mysticism. I refer to that contrast which has already come to our attention. The contrast is between two conceptions of what constitutes communion with God. On the one hand we have the conception that communion with the divine reaches its culmination in pure ecstatic enjoyment, or in pure indifference as in Nirvana, in which the personal, conscious, and volitional life flows out and loses itself as the river in the ocean. On

[46] [Rasmus Nielsen (1809-1884), Danish philosophy professor who tried to supplement Kierkegaard with a philosophy of reason. He argued that reason and faith could get along together because they were so different.]

[47] E. Lehman, "En tysk Bog og en dansk Betragtning," *Teologisk Tidskrift,* IV (1903), 282.

the other hand we have the conception of communion with God which culminates in the meeting of the prophets with the living God, or in the union of Christ with the Father. The latter conception re-created the personality of the prophets and conveyed new thoughts and new superhuman powers for their task (Jer. 1).

The appraisal will be determined by the difference in personal attitudes. Without doubt the prophetic religious experience, with its knowledge of God as a living, active, personal or super-personal almighty power, the Lord of life and history, presents a far more difficult problem for our thought than does the methodical absorption of the soul into the dim and distant depths of being. But no attentive observer can deny the characteristic difference. It is found most clearly in the great personalities, who have been founders of religions. One can compare the prophets of Israel with the great souls, for the most part unnamed, which speak to us in the Upanishads. The supremacy of India in the art of effecting union with the Infinite and in perfecting the theories of this art, was observed already by the ancients. Philostratus puts in the mouth of Appolonius of Tyana the words, "that all wish to live in the nearness of God, but only the Hindus really bring it to pass." Compare, for example, Jesus with Buddha! The difference between them according to the comparison made above can thus be expressed: Jesus is a prophet, Buddha a mystic. According to the latter comparison thus: Jesus is the perfect revealer of God, the Son of God, the God-man; Buddha is the guide to Nirvana! But the two types do not end with these alone. They are continuous also in the many religious personalities of the second, third, and fourth order, who confess themselves dependent on the great ones. Because the mysterious, the indivisible, and the inexplicable is found in both, we feel constrained to name them both mysticism, and differentiate between them by calling the one the *mysticism of personality* and the other the mysticism of nature, or perhaps better the *mysticism of infinity*.[48]

[48] Cf. my "Nutidsbildning och kristlig innerlighet," in *Förhandlingarna vid studentmötet i Sorö* (1903); reprinted in *När stunderna växla och skrida* (Saml. 1; Stockholm, 1909), pp. 63-89.

The difference lies in the role which the personal life plays. The question is, must the personal life be repressed or extinguished in order to gain the end of religion or attain its higher stages? Or shall it be re-created and purified, so that the natural ego is surrendered and the eternal loving union with God, the "image of God" of theology, the "soul spark" (*Funkelein*) of the German mysticism of the Middle Ages, is realized and grows into a new man, the man of God, the concentrated and active life of love in an ethical personality? Is the way to knowledge of the divine the way of negation (*via negationis*), which leads, as Plotinus says, to the other side of existence, to where the "soul without being good or evil or anything," without consciousness of body or spirit, receives the divine? Must we, with Hierotheus, reach "the mysterious, silent stillness, which dissolves consciousness and form," or again, with the Areopagite, or Eckhart, or Ruysbroek, arrive at "the divine darkness," "the nameless, formless nothing."[49] Or, is the way to God a way of affirmation (*via positionis*), which leads through a complete self-renunciation and self-denial to a richer and stronger personal life; to the revelation of the divine will of love in the most glowing, most perfect and most nobly formed personal life, that of Jesus Christ? This way reveals its presence by many good and wonderful gifts, but nowhere is it nearer God nor does it ever know a higher attitude toward God and a richer fullness of God than in the highest endowment of life: personal love built on the foundation of a living trust in God. This love is a warm, human reality, whether in suffering or in jubilant joy. It is entirely different from the self-sacrifice of mysticism, which is at bottom a cold thing, although it is capable of complete renunciation without complaint or even of suffering martyrdom in flames at the stake (I Cor. 12 and 13). Is God the great, silent sea of infinity, which yearns to have the individual broken fragments float together again, formless and nameless, to slumber in its mysterious embrace? Or is God the overmastering, enkindling, and burning holy love, which wills and

[49] W. R. Inge, *Christian Mysticism* (New York: Scribner's, 1899), pp. 97, 103, 182.

generates personal life? Is he not interpreted to us only in a personal life of love, so that the word will be true which says, "Outside this human being God is not to be found (*Extra hunc hominem nullus Deus reperitus*)?" Are we not nearest him and most like him when we rejoice in our personal life and in the attainment of the deepest self by losing the selfish ego?

The vindication of personality in this sense is the very opposite of a self-glorifying demand for the rights of the individual. Harald Hjärne, the Swedish historian, in an essay on Lafcadio Hearn,[50] the American revealer of Japan, points out the complete misconception which this Greek-Irish-North American has of the solidarity of Japanese society. Lafcadio Hearn, in his antipathy against the noisy individualism and dogmatic lordship of the Western world, has confused this solidarity which is founded on religion with what Hjärne calls "the cloud-kingdom of impersonal mysticism." Hjärne writes: "He is mistaken—we can safely say so on the basis of his own testimony. What he has seen is not the destruction of personality, but its resurrection into a richer life in an unbroken continuity with a rejuvenated society. From the depths of magic there emerge only powers of darkness, which bind the conscious and responsible life of the spirit. Any will power which is directed to higher things is never a drive toward extinction of the personal life. It is the very core of personality, which is strengthened more and more in the degree in which the call to higher things is heard and becomes more clear. Every social community is built upon the foundation of a personal, self-sacrificing will. If the foundation is undermined the building will fall. The height to which the structure can rise is conditioned in the sustaining strength of the foundation. All history, that of the ancient world and of our own forefathers, bears testimony to this fact."

Two points of contrast between revealed religion and the reli-

[50] [Lafcadio Hearn (1850-1904) was an American lecturer in English at Tokyo University who wrote a dozen books on Japan of which at least six were translated into Swedish. That the renowned historian Harald Hjärne and Söderblom should give special attention to him indicates the vogue which he enjoyed in Sweden. In the original volume this entire paragraph constituted a footnote.]

gion of mysticism are connected with this difference which we have above indicated. First, as to personal authority. The religious relation of one person to another in the mysticism of infinity, becomes at best something impersonal, a prescription, an indication, an illumination, knowledge of the way to attain experience. The influence and authority of great personalities play a very important role in the mysticism of infinity, it is true, for such are the necessary conditions in human life. But this influence of personalities is really fundamentally antagonistic to the essence of a mysticism which transcends time and history. Within the trinity of Buddhism *dhamma*, doctrine or direction, is without doubt the most important element.[51] The heroes of the highest religious development of the Greeks, Socrates, Plato, and Plotinus, reject all claim to be authorities. They do this in the interest of purity in the relation to God. Christian mysticism also has felt that a personal, religious relation to Jesus Christ, as shown in the Gospels and in history, was a burden and an imperfection. "Mysticism is a specific form of religion, namely a piety which feels that the historical in the positive religions is a burden from which it would free itself" (W. Herrmann). "The Bible is a safeguard against all mysticism which is alien toward history. Mysticism would know only of the innermost immediacy in relation to God. Feeling and imagination alone are valid as organs of the religious life. Society and history are viewed as hindrances to the religious life and must, so much as possible, be rejected in favor of the inner life" (M. Kähler).[52] In the Bible itself the problem of these differences comes to light. The attempt is made to solve it by the short cut of mystical religion. But the problem which is made actual by the critical investigation of the Scriptures proves to be too complex for such an easy solution. Mysticism eludes the ancient and fundamental Christian question: How can we reconcile the fact that Christianity is indissolubly joined to a phenomenon in time, namely,

---

[51] Cf. my book *Treenigheten* (Uppsala: 1903), pp. 16 ff.

[52] [Martin Kähler (1835-1912), German theologian, professor in Halle. For an exposition of his thought see *The So-Called Historical Jesus and the Historic, Biblical Christ,* trans. and edited by Carl E. Braaten (Philadelphia: Fortress, 1964). His influence in Sweden seems to have been considerable, especially on Einar Billing.]

the indispensable authority of Jesus, with the claim that Christianity is the absolute religion, exalting the religious relation above all risks of relativity?[53]

Within the revealed religion personal authority is an integral part of religion and is recognized as such. This is true already of the Old Testament prophets. Revelation is bound up with their personalities. Wellhausen has with his keen insight seen this. He says: "It belongs to the prophetic, the genuine idea of revelation, that Jahweh, above and beyond all ordered mediation, communicates himself to the individual, the chosen one, in whom the mysterious, indivisible relation in which the Deity stands to human beings is exalted and becomes active. Apart from the prophets, that is, *in abstracto,* there can be no revelation. Revelation exists for and in the human ego. Hereby arises the synthesis of seeming contradictions. The subjective in its highest significance, exalted above all rules, is the truly objective, the divine."

This connection between religion and the chosen men of God was not broken in the progress of development, so that it cannot be consider a lower, pedagogical measure. Rather, in the history of religion, the unheard of has happened, which has created the paradox of Christianity. Revealed religion has reached its perfection, not in a perfect doctrine or guide to salvation, but in a person. "For other foundation can no man lay than that which is laid, which is Jesus Christ." In this person the divine and human, the objective and the subjective are fused. He stands at the same time "as the perfection of divine love and of human faithfulness" (Frederick Fehr),[54] and mediates the communion of his own with God. The principle of personality is the strength of evangelical Christianity. It knows only one authority, the authority of personality.[55]

[53] The problem has been set in all its bearings in the important work of E. Troeltsch, *Die Absolutheit des Christentums und die Religiongeschichte* (Tübingen: Mohr, 1912).

[54] [Frederik Fehr (1849-1895), the first Swedish theologian to espouse Ritschl's theology.]

[55] Cf. Harald Höffding, *Religionsfilosofi* (Copenhagen: Det Nordiske förlag, 1901), pp. 241 ff., 275 ff. If the lines of thought which he presents are drawn out to their conclusions, which they are not, they lead to the authority of the evangelical religion, the personal authority of Jesus.

In the second place, mystical religion in the abstract sense is attainable only for the upper ten thousand of spiritual culture and refinement. Only they have the time and the ability to procure for themselves the experience in question. Mystic religions are essentially aristocratic and must be decked out in an exoteric garment if they are to be accessible to those "who labor and are heavy laden."

Jesus praises his heavenly Father because he has hidden this from the wise and revealed it unto babes. To have a vision of God requires a pure heart and a clear and true personality, not knowledge, not an art or a method. To know him there is needed the heart of a child, not philosophy. The prophets and Jesus addressed themselves to the conscience, to the elementary ethical censor in man. They depend upon its sanction. The sign which Jesus gave was the sign of Jonah, the sign of the prophet, of the preaching of repentance. Artificiality is the worst hindrance of the gospel. Jesus cannot tolerate Pharisees, but he goes in to eat with sinners and publicans. The authority of his apostles was not based on extraordinary experiences, although they possessed such. They offered their credentials thus: "by the manifestation of the truth commending ourselves to every man's conscience in the sight of God."[56]

Two misconceptions must here be removed. Ethical elements are not lacking in the mysticism of nature and the mysticism of infinity. On the contrary, the ethical is given a more and more prominent place in the process of "purification," in those means by which communion with God is brought about. This is true beyond as well as within Christianity, in India, in Platonism, Neoplatonism, Sufism, and the mysticism of the Middle Ages.[57] But here the actual communion with God is affected "beyond good and evil" (*jenseits von Gut und Böse*). It is not that the personal life in its fullness of ethical character and vital energy is filled and strengthened. It is repressed in this communion with God. In the religion of the monks, which is a mysticism of infinity, personality entirely disap-

---

[56] [II Cor. 4:2.]
[57] W. R. Inge, *Christian Mysticism.*

pears. It is not simply chance that in the first order of monks which Pachomius gathered, the brethren were designated and classified by the letters of the alphabet.[58] Ethics becomes an ascetic practice, a self-discipline for the purpose of transcending every "creaturely" thing not a direct service of God with a positive end, the kingdom of God. The Reformers could make the accusation against their opponents that they were not able to say how the Holy Spirit is given and how good works are produced. William James is right when he points out that no one and nothing in Roman Catholic theology can speak with such a heart for sick souls as does Martin Luther.

And further, the difference between the mysticism of personality and the mysticism of infinity does not imply that unusual, abnormal physical and psychical phenomena, such as visions and ecstatic conditions, are banished from the former. God can permit his power and love to be revealed in heavenly visions and notable raptures. Decisive experiences in revealed religion can be clothed in such forms. The disciples on the Mount of Transfiguration and Paul on the road to Damascus are proofs of this. Many of the prophets had clairvoyant and passionate experiences of soul, such as characterized the Canaanite *nebiim*. Others had none.[59] Such experiences are not restricted to the period of revelation, but appear in our day in the experiences of many Christians, in proportion to their personal endowments and the ways of God. S. Michelet calls attention to the revelation given Hans Nielsen Hauge,[60] on April 5, 1796. Many other examples can be given. But the difference between these and the experiences of the other forms of mystical religion is clear.

1. In the revealed religion the extraordinary states of soul are

[58] L. Moltesen, *Det Kristne Munkvoesen* (1901), p. 104.

[59] S. Michelet, "Israels profeter som åbenbaringens boerere," in *Religonisvetenskapliga kongressens i Stockholm förhandlingar* (1897), pp. 494 ff. [German trans., *Israels Propheten als Träger der offenbarung* (Tübingen: J. C. B. Mohr, 1898)]. Mohammed was a visionary, but was anxious not to be classed with the professional ecstatics of his day.

[60] [Hans Nielsen Hauge (1771-1824) was a Norwegian lay preacher whose orthodox and pietistic preaching resulted in a widespread revival movement in Norway which was transplanted to this country through immigrants.]

lacking entirely in some of the greatest personalities. I am not now exclusively concerned with the fact that there is related of Jesus no ecstatic feature, still less ecstasy in a technical sense, for Jesus has a place all his own. The greatest of the prophets, Jeremiah, lacks every trace of ectasy. Neither did Luther have any ecstatic experiences.

2. Where they are found, they are never adduced as a necessary condition of attaining communion with God, nor are they claimed to be the highest or the essential thing in religion. St. Paul is forced to overcome his modesty when he tells of his visions and revelations in the second letter to the Corinthians. In I Corinthians 12:31 and chapter 13 he makes up the table of precedence and put love above such extraordinary manifestations as that of speaking with tongues.

Ecstatic experiences occur in all nature-religions as the highest and essential communion with God. At lower stages this is manifested in violent forms, at higher stages in purer and nobler forms, For practical purposes, for guidance in religion, the most ancient form of a psychology of religion comes to light even in the nature-religions. In India and Greece the conditions and stages of the ecstatic experience were studied and described with extraordinary penetration and refinement. Those who noted them have become the teachers both of the Eastern and of the Western world, in the East in Sufism, in the West in Christian mysticism. Historical and literary influence is evident. But because of the fact that human nature is everywhere the same, the Jacob's ladder of ecstasy everywhere becomes essentially the same, even though no influence of one religion upon another has taken place.[61] In its most refined form ecstasy, in the truest sense, is a most exalted and refined enjoyment of the infinite. It is vastly different from the sensual, emotional intoxication of the lower forms of mysticism. It tends on

[61] The mysticism of infinity is everywhere similar. Maeterlinck in *Le Tresor des Humbles* finds that Ruysbroek "although he did not know it was influenced by Platonism in Greece, Sufism in Persia, Brahmanism in India and Buddhism in Thibet." W. R. Inge, *Christian Mysticism,* pp. 171 f.

analysis to evaporate. Ecstasy, in the truest sense, is an experience outside of consciousness. It nowise corresponds to that which in common parlance is summed up under the term "ecstatic experience." It is not the same as St. Paul's experience which he describes in II Corinthians 12, for he remembered what he had heard and seen.

3. Ecstasy in the proper sense of the word, which is the goal of the mysticism of infinity, is unthinkable as a form for the higher experience of revealed religion. For revealed religion includes knowledge of the living God and a revelation of his nature. Ecstasy on the other hand, shuts out all positive knowledge and every communication of truth. We must not, in the interest of rationality, set aside and disregard the extraordinary mental states through which God communicates with man according to his good pleasure. Proofs in favor of extraordinary experiences and the mystery of religion[62] are heartily welcome to counteract the weight which we lay upon the satisfaction of the mind. Still, it would be a poor corrective to fall into nature mysticism. Whatever of holy memories God may wish to afford, in quiet or in great raptures, in voices, in visions, which will shine through and illuminate the whole of life, this is his good pleasure. We must not, however, build the religious life on the basis of that which cannot and must not be mentally grasped. We must not exchange the valuation which St. Paul has given us for that of the mysticism of infinity.

Within that complex religious creation which is called Christianity, not only the prophetic religion but also the Aryan nature-religion and culture-religion were continued, although its mysticism of infinity received a strong Christian modification. In part this consisted in the consciousness of the living God, which was an active inheritance from the gospel, while consistency with the point of view of the past tended toward pantheism and abstract idealism. In part it consisted in visionary elements taken from a conception of Christ which was more or less detached from history. And finally it

[62] B. Duhm, *Das Geheimnis in der Religion* (Leipzig: Mohr, 1896).

consisted partly in Christian ethics. Within Christianity as it developed, the two chief types of the cultivation of the inner life can be studied. There is a mixed form with a manifold of nuances which we find in such mystics as the Areopagite, Bernard, Meister Eckhart, Theresa, Wordsworth, and Amiel. Then there are such personal mystics as Augustine (who returned finally to the Christian impressions of his childhood), Luther, Pascal, John Bunyan, Vinet, Kierkegaard, Wikner. Luther himself had been fascinated by the mystic religion, the genuine, noble flower of the Middle Ages, which lived its life of imperishable beauty in the very midst of doctrines of works, sacramental magic, worldly ambitions for power, and the weeds of decadence. We remember the warm recommendation which Luther gave the *German Theology*, which he published in its entirety in 1518. Later on, Luther had to meet a different manifestation of mysticism in Carlstadt and the prophets of Zwickau, who held an unevangelical doctrine of a contradiction between soul and body, between the inner and the outer life, and had gone over to the side of legalism. When Luther, in opposition to these, developed his own doctrine of liberty through Christ in faith and love,[63] in his zeal he made no distinction between the *Schwärmer* and the mystics who were true to the best traditions of mysticism. In this he was unjust.

It is clear that Luther, with the exclusiveness, the prepossession, which sometimes characterizes religious genius, was not then able to see that the mystic religion was another basic type with legitimate claims in its species, possessed of beauty and truth and feeling. He could not see that it was at home in the world of inner warmth and devotion to God.

Luther has with incomparable richness and clarity described "the communion of the Christian with God" according to the character of revealed religion, as contrasted with the sublime mysticism of infinity. Faith and confidence are expressions of personal relations.

---

[63] *Glaube und liebe* is the constantly recurring theme in the tract *Wider die himmlischen Propheten* [*Against the Heavenly Prophets*, in *Luther's Works*, American edition, Vol. 40 (Philadelphia: Muhlenberg, 1958), pp. 73-224].

Through basing his faith on Christ, on the revelation of God, and not on any ambiguous or uncertain experiences of his own in the form of a mystical emotional life or of a fulfilling of the law, Luther won his certainty of salvation. In this assurance of salvation and in the doctrine of the intimate connection of the new life with faith, Luther has indicated the distinguishing mark of personal religion, for the humblest Christian man as well as for great and chosen souls. In a clear and simple way he has shown the victory over mysticism and, as well, over legal religion.[64] He says of his opponents: "They nowhere teach how we can be rid of sin, receive a good conscience, and win a peaceful and happy heart before God, which is the most important of all."

As against the "enthusiasts," the *Schwärmer*, Luther has also pointed out a psychological mark of identification of the religious experience which belongs to the mysticism of personality. This is the *terrores conscientiae*, the terror of conscience (*Frygt og Baeven* of Kierkegaard), a phrase which, with precision, defines the difference between his religion and the mysticism of infinity and marks the personal, ethical character of the former and its consciousness of the power of God. I quote Luther's letter to Melanchthon, January 13, 1522. He urges Melanchthon to test the alleged prophets. He was to question them to ascertain "if they have any experience of spiritual tribulations and the divine birth pangs, death and hell. If you hear only of pleasant delights, of tranquility, devotion (as they will call it), and piety, you must discredit them, even if they claim to have been exalted to the third heaven." Because of the weight I attach to the following text, I quote it in the original.

> *Quaeras, num experti sint spirituales illas angustias et nativitates divinas, mortes, infernosque. Si audieris blanda, tranquilla, devota (ut vocant) et religiosa, etiamsi in tertium coelum sese raptos dicant, non approbabis.* Quia signum filii hominis deest, qui est βασανος,

---

[64] See the discussion of the subject by A. Harnack in *Dogmengeschichte* (Tübingen: Mohr, 1914) [cf. Vol. 7 of the English trans., *History of Dogma* (New York: Russell and Russell, 1959), p. 184].

probator unicus Christianorum et certus spirituum descretor. Vis scire locum, tempus, modum colloquiorum divinorum? audi: *sicut leo contrivit omnia ossa, et projectus sum a facie oculorum tuorum, et repleta est malis anima mea, et vita mea inferno appropinquavit.* Non sic loquitor Majestas (ut vocant) immediate, ut homo videat, imo, *non videbit me homo, et vivet.* Et stellam parvam sermonis ejus non fert natura. Ideo enim per homines loquitur, quod loquentum ipsum ferre omnes non possumus. Nam et virginem turbavit angelus, sic et Danielem, *sic et Jermias queritur: corripe me in judicio, et non sis tu mihi formidini.* Et quid plura? Quasi Majestas possit cum vetere homine loqui familiariter, et non prius occidere atque exsic-care, ne foeteant odores ejus pessimi, cum sit ignis consumens. Etiam somnia et visiones sanctorum sunt terribiles saltem, postquam in-telliguntur. Tenta ergo et ne Iesum quidem audias glorisum, nisi videris prius crucifixum.[65]

It is true that this word about terrors of conscience, *terrores conscientiae,* which Melanchthon, not from his own experience but from Luther's, has made a part of the *Apology of the Augsburg Confession* of 1531 and set up as the necessary condition for cer-tainty of faith, has caused confusion and led to a certain unnatural-ness in Lutheran piety. One must concede that Spener is right when he says that experience differs among Christians. "With some the process is more lenient. The power of the law is hardly felt before the comfort of the Gospel heals all."[66] It is wrong and unpsycho-

---

[65] "For the sign of the Son of Man is lacking, which is the touchstone, the only mark of a Christian, and the sure divider of the spirits. Would you know the place, the time, and the manner of conversation with God, listen: 'The lion crushes all their bones' (Dan. 6:24): 'My soul is full of troubles and my life draweth near to Sheol' (Ps. 88:3). The Divine Majesty does not speak, as they say, immediately, so that a man may see it. Nay, 'no man can see me and live' (Exod. 33:20). Human nature cannot endure even a little of the speech of God. He speaks through men, for we could not endure the speaker himself. Even the Virgin was terrified by the angel. So also Daniel. And Jeremiah cries: 'Correct me, O Lord, but in moderation' (Jer. 10:24). 'Be not a terror unto me' (17:17). And what more? As though the Divine Majesty could speak intimately with the 'old man' and not first kill it or dry it up, so that its worst smells may not stink when the fire consumes it. Even the dreams and visions of the saints are terrifying, when they are understood. Examine and you will find that not even Jesus was exalted before he was crucified." [A translation of the letter is given in *Luther's Works,* American edition, Vol. 48 (Philadelphia: Fortress, 1963), pp. 364-72.]
[66] A. Ritschl, *Geschichte des Pietismus,* Vol. II (Bonn: A. Marcus, 1886), p. 113.

logical to make the experience of the great hero of faith the standard for all. The penalty has been paid in the mechanization of repentance and a lapse into emotional and legal religion.

On the other hand it will not do to explain, as do Ritschl and Harnack, the *terrores conscientiae* of Luther, his "spiritual tribulations" (*angustias spirituales*), his experience of "death and hell" (*mortes et infernos*), as being caused by his individual situation and the ignorance of salvation in which his church had held him. Such experiences are not peculiar to Luther. They are found also in men of God of revealed religion in the Holy Scriptures, on whom Luther builds in the letter quoted. They have been verified by many, known and unknown, since his day. Even today they are often marks of a deep and vital religious experience. They are not necessarily the result of reflection on the sense of guilt, but they are the reaction of the whole human personality to the infinite holiness and majesty of God.

Luther does not exclude extraordinary and ecstatic experiences of those who have real communion with the living God. He speaks implicitly of "the dreams and visions of the saints." They are neither made necessary conditions nor are they excluded. Herein is revealed the spiritual and ethical character of the mysticism of personality. In the mysticism of infinity the highest and essential communion with God is bound up with a carefully specified physical and psychic preparation, namely, ecstasy. A refined and ethereal, but not invisible, remnant from the primitive nature-religion is thus revealed in the ennobled religious self-discipline of culture-religion.

The words of Luther to Melanchthon, who was less at home in the depths of spiritual experience, give us a firm grasp on the psychological distinction between the two types of religious experience. The identifying marks of the mysticism of infinity are "pleasant delights, tranquillity, devotion, piety" (*blanda, tranquilla, devota et religiosa*). St. Francis heard the angel drawing the bow across the strings of the celestial violin. The infinite sweetness and beauty of the tone was such that one more stroke would have brought him death in complete blessedness. The mysticism of infinity in its pure form seeks its way out to the point of union with the divine by leaving, by degrees, the creaturely, divesting itself of all qualities, pushing slowly out beyond the sole distinction of existence and nonexistence, being and nonbeing. Beyond the last cliffs of conscious life lies the goal, wrapped in mist. It is without space and form, without name and outline that can be remembered. The moments spent in genuine ecstasy cannot even be described, for consciousness is extinguished. They are surrounded by an inexpressible sanctity and given an ethereal fragrance. During the time that Porphyrios abode with his admired master, Plotinus four times experienced union with that divine life which is in all that exists.[67] The purest element of ecstasy consists in a liberty, won step by step, until the outermost limits of life are reached.

How different is the world of personal mysticism! Jeremiah, St. Paul, Augustine, Luther, Pascal, Kierkegaard, cry out: "Lord, spare me! Depart from me! My guilt!" (*O, culpa mea!*) The miserable human creature quakes and shivers, bleeds and moans. In mysticism of infinity we see an outstretched hand, a longing, dreaming gaze. In the mysticism of personality we see a man who shrinks back in dread and dares not even lift up his eyes. In the former there is an ascension, in the latter a struggle in the darkness of death. Under the mighty grasp of God the recipient of God's grace shudders. He cannot escape and he would not escape. He kisses and blesses the hand of God, for it lifts him up into another world, into the blessed kingdom of life and so holds him secure, so safe, that he can defy sin and death and the devil. In the former we have liberty in the dim spaces of infinity; in the latter, liberty in the mighty hand of God. In the former a struggle toward the One, the great and unutterable One; in the latter, a meeting in quiet places perhaps, but also in the desert, in labor, with an attacking, living, active will; with an overflowing, empowering fullness of personal

---

[67] *Vita Plotini* XXIII [Porphyry's *Life of Plotinus* is included in Vol. 1 of *Plotinus,* trans. from Greek to English by Stephen Mackenna (6 vols.; London: Medici Society, 1917-1930)].

life of holiness and love, in comparison with which all else that is called life is but a disappointment, an illusion. In the one, the great stillness, the distant unfathomable depths of divinity; in the other, a living God, unutterably active, who crushes us, but also saves us.

I shall not carry further this comparison between the ecstatic enjoyment and the *terrores* and *angustiae* of personal mysticism. As we study the peculiar and meaningful forms of communion with God both within and outside revealed religion, we cannot escape the strong impression that, in the mysticism of personality, God conducts himself, if I may speak thus naively and in human ways about the activity of the unfathomable God, in a manner entirely different from that observed in the other. He is active, intervening, self-communicating, attacking, revealing, standing forth in the life of the soul as in the world of history.[68] All this is on the supposition that we feel obliged to make the metaphysical venture of faith from the subjective experiences of the human soul to God and his work. If we proceed from experience to the Experienced One, we find that a part of the field of the inner life detaches itself and is marked as the area of a *special revelation of God*.

Ecstasy in its highest sense does not characterize the important and essential experiences of personal mysticism. Tribulations (*angustiae*) and terrors (*terrores*) are foreign to genuine mysticism of infinity. Yet, we are mindful of the fact that there is one, and only one, who possesses and transmits at the burning center of his personal life of love the infinite fullness of God's being. This one is Jesus Christ. In the unsearchable purity of his communion with the Father he does not show a sign of ecstasy, but neither does he show *terrores* and *angustiae*, such as men of God before and since his time have felt. Gethsemane and Golgotha are places of anguish beyond all anguish, distress beyond all distresses. But never do we hear from his lips, "O my guilt!"

The Christian church cannot build its certainty of possessing the

[68] Cf. E. G. Geijer, *Föreläsningar över människans historia,* in his *Samlade Skrifter,* Vol. II, pt. 2 (Stockholm: P. A. Norstedt, 1875), p. 217.

revelation of God, the word of God through prophets and through Christ, on the results of historical and psychological investigation. The church cannot wait in uncertainty until this investigation is completed. She builds her assurance on her own experience and testimony, verified by every regenerate soul. The same is true for dogmatic theology, which is the scientific interpretation of the self-consciousness of the church.[69] It is, however, of supreme importance that the claims which underlie such a certainty be investigated in the light of the entire historical reality of religion on our earth. It is then revealed in a surprising way that the certainty of revelation which the church possesses is not reduced to that kind of certainty which every other religion claims for its object. Instead it is found that there is a very deep and marked difference within the world of religion itself as it is revealed in history and in the inner life of the soul. The science of religion has not as yet got its eye fixed on this specific line of demarcation in the history of religion. It is still so dazzled by its own variegated and rich field of labor, so full of joy at having attained its liberty from the bondage of ecclesiastical formulations—a liberty which has brought welfare and comfort not to itself alone, but to the church as well—that it has not discovered this boundary line. Ultimately the fact of this difference will gain attention and make possible a far more detailed investigation than these pages afford.

This distinction, however, must not be pressed too far. Our human understanding is so constituted that for purposes of study we must separate that which in reality is interwoven. Let us sum up our findings. The history of religion reveals to us two types of communion with God. In the one, the subject considers the goal of religion to be reached in the loss of self. I and Thou are to become identical. The climax in this mysticism is reached in the soul of man becoming identified with deity. *Tat tvam asi.* ("I am God.") The other form attains communion with God by losing the self, the

[69] Cf. L. Ihmels, *Die Selbständigkeit der Dogmatik gegenüber der Religionsphilosophie* (Leipzig: Deichert, 1901).

limited, selfish ego, but not by extinction, submergence in the sea of infinity, but through realizing its true nature in God. There is in this communion no cessation of communicated interchange between an I and the Thou. The soul is mastered by the majesty of God, by his power and grace, so that it is no longer able to speak or distinguish clearly. The depth of spiritual communion finds at last no words, no adequate expression for its reality. Here also is an ecstasy, an exaltation above the conscious. But the unity with the divine is one of fellowship of the human and the divine, not of absorption and extinction of the human in the divine.

We find these two types of religion in some instances in a pure form. But in most cases we can trace something of the one and of the other in the same individual. The fundamental difference comes to light when either discipline and absorption becomes the chief end, or else the revelation and intervention of God.

2

THE PORTALS OF REVELATION

When we speak of revelation[1] in this connection, it cannot mean anything less than knowledge of the essential nature of reality. It must be added, however, that it means also an insight, a penetration, which satisfies not only a more or less powerful intellectual faculty in us, but which gives to our very being that point of contact it needs for its vital power, for salvation, and for the realization of our true dignity.

Revelation means still more. The word has something to say about the manner in which this knowledge is imparted. Revelation implies that man is the one who receives, God the one who communicates himself. Seers and wise men, and ordinary religious persons as well, have in all ages and in widely separated religions borne testimony to the experience of the self-communication of the divine, to the certainty of truth, of God, of the spirit, of salvation. They have also testified that this comes as a gift. There must be a search, it is true, but revelation is not something which can be seized as booty but is received without price. Obviously we have here to do with a psychological fact, verified also outside the area of religion, within that of creative art. Insight comes instantaneously. Certainty spreads through the mind like a light from heaven. The truth shines forth like lightning. But when we here speak of revelation, we are not satisfied with merely recognizing such a way of working of the human soul. If such a breaking forth of clarity and certainty is nothing more than a particular form of the psychic proc-

[1] Cf. my *Religionsproblemet inom katolicism och protestantism,* Vol. II (Stockholm, 1910).

ess, we cannot know whether or not we have to do with a deeper reality. The word revelation would then be used not in a real sense and would not necessarily correspond to reality.

Here we are met by the great problem, always in the center of the battle, either denied or affirmed: Can we have any knowledge of supersensual reality in or behind that which our senses perceive? Are we helplessly shut out from a real revelation because of the very nature of our means of knowledge? Or is it possible for us to possess communication with the spiritual world?

In regard to this problem, which has been and is being answered in different ways by philosophy, I shall point out two actual facts. The variation of views in this matter stands in close relation to the drift of the age and its ruling methods of work. The tendency to deny the possibility of revelation may be due to a certain fatigue of the intellect after an epoch of great daring in metaphysical thought. Or else it may arise out of the fact that the demands of our civiliza tion direct the attention and labor so energetically and exclusively to that which is nearest at hand, to the investigation and practical application of our material resources, the facts of history, and the investigation of the human mind, that there is no strength left for metaphysics, for the questions concerning the real meaning of our existence, which are capable of so many interpretations. For a considerable time, yet not for all time, can this attitude of concern only for that which the eye can see convey so strong an impression of the massive solidity of material things that the spiritual reality seems like a world of mist and dreams. It cannot be for long. Only give the human intellect time enough and science will itself dissolve this seemingly compact and solid reality into symbols and signs upon which the human spirit can never find rest and build a real insight into truth, a faith and a conviction.

The generations immediately preceding ours, and we ourselves, have lived through a period in which metaphysical problems have been thrust aside, both because of fatigue after the heat of an age of creative effort, and also because of an intensive concentration on the empirical and technical perhaps unique in the history of civilization. We are now experiencing along the whole line a double phenomenon. On the one hand, we are not satisfied with merely using the methods of natural science to benefit mankind by inventions and by the art and technique of medicine and surgery. We are examining the worth and the meaning of knowledge itself. And this is being done not only by professional philosophers and critics in the field of the knowledge process. Even those who pursue the exact and the descriptive sciences turn about and examine their own methods asking: What can these methods, these experiments and theories really give us, and what are they unable to give? From all this has come the insight that the basic theories of natural science have meaning and value only in the degree in which they are conceived as tools for the control of nature, but that they become contradictory if one expects through them to arrive at knowledge of what reality truly is. No one can halt at the mere insight and hypotheses of natural science in certainty, silent or expressed, that we have found in the atoms or in the ether the mystery of reality. The critical examination of science itself has driven the scientists of our day out of such a position.

But not only this. At the same time there has come a great wave of interest in the problem of reality itself. Where are we and whither are we moving? Can we be certain of anything? If we can, what is the nature of that reality upon which our thought and faith can obtain a foothold? I am not thinking now of the bizarre and curious oddities in which, not seldom, metaphysics has taken refuge when thrust to one side. I am thinking of the newly awakened metaphysical interest and a fresh confidence which characterizes the critical thinking of our day. We cannot and we will not be satisfied agnostically to renounce any positive certainty, just as little as we can any longer be rocked to sleep in an uncritical dogmatism of metaphysics. The tendency of the thought of the age is to inquire as to the possibility, yes, to feel the vital necessity of insight into the nature of reality itself. But we have lost much of our confidence in the methods of knowledge with which both rational idealism and materialism have worked.

Before I proceed to the three fundamental phenomena in human personality in which revelation has chiefly been sought or recognized and from which, according to my conviction, it issues, there is needed a word about the approximative or symbolic character of our understanding of what revelation is. I am not here pleading for skepticism. On the contrary, I shall maintain in what follows that an assured certainty can be reached which, together with a clearly defined form, belong to the very essence of revelation. But we must give over the habit of reasoning about the mystery of reality and of God, as though it were like the question of an equation, or of the politics of the Kaiser, or of the canals of Mars. How insipid and pretentious some ways of treating the greatest of all problems must appear to any one who has had a vital appreciation of the rich and mysterious, the imposing and unfathomable complexity into which we enter as but infinitesimal elements. Examples of clear and firm attitudes toward life, of unswerving convictions, such that a man could die for them, assuredly do not involve also the ability adequately to express them. How have not prophets and apostles felt that! We, creeping creatures of earth, seek to grasp in comprehensive symbols the decisive experiences which history and life give us. Human would-be wisdom easily conceals under a prudent logical precision the lack of genuine, vital experience. Instead of that urgent and intimate contact with reality which alone brings salvation with insight into truth, there is substituted a sort of juggling with terms and symbols, which in its self-confidence loses the thing itself, exchanging it for an empty form. The feeling of the wonderful and inconceivable riches which lie behind all our terms for the divine should keep alive our consciousness of the provisional, the incomplete character of these terms. The usefulness and transparency of the symbols does not mean that they are perfectly grasped rationally. It means that we ought never—I say never—to use them—God, reality, truth, heavenly Father, the personality of God, being, life—unless the miracle of reality shimmers through them. If dust and grime are permitted to collect on these windows—for that is what these religious terms of ours are—or, if we actually paint them over to keep the light from blinding us we no longer will discern anything of that spiritual world which they would reveal to us. Instead we see only them, the signs instead of the things signified, the windows instead of the light and the figure they are meant to transmit. Beyond question we have lost out of much of our spiritual language, old and new, learned and unlearned, that background of reality which alone transforms the words from empty sounds (which really means that we profane and blaspheme holy things) into participation in reality and life.

Even when we stand before a human being we can perceive how utterly impossible it is for us to express the reality of his being or to put it into a comprehensive formula or term. How much more difficult must it be to fix in words, which of course only can be symbols—because the thing is beyond the senses—the conviction of the basic power of reality, or God. This does not by any means imply that we can be careless or uncertain as to the terms we use for reality, as if it could be represented to us in almost any way you please, or as if you may exchange one symbol for another, as, for example, impersonality for personality in the being of God, or dualism for monism in our own religious views. No indeed, an absolute certainty can easily be combined with a vital feeling that it is incomprehensible. Such we find that St. Paul possessed in relation to the being and ways of God.

The portals for revelation in the human personality are three: the intellect or understanding, the intuition of infinity, with its emphasis on feeling, and the urge of the ideal, or the conscience. The three are by no means of equal value.

I

We have already spoken of the very restricted use of the intellect as a source of knowledge of reality. Modern critical science harks back in different ways to Kant. But he was by no means the first to show the limited sphere of the intellect. The great thinkers and religious men of all times, Plato and Plotinus, St. Paul and St. Augustine, Luther and Pascal, and Hindu thinkers as well, have given expression to the experience that insight into the being of reality does not come through the analyzing investigation and logical conclusions of the understanding, but rather through intuition, through surrender to authority, through will and faith. Culture reveals that if the intellect is allowed to exert a one-sided rule to the exclusion of other powers in human life the result is a dissolution of certainty and also of initiative, of personal as well as communal vitality. Reality is dissolved into misty vagueness. If the intellect is depended upon as a source of truth, as being able to satisfy the thirst for pure truth and to reveal the essence of reality, it will be found, on the one hand, to be impotent by reason of its abstractness, or, on the other hand, to be liable to lead us astray and to dissolve all certainty. If we conceive it, however, as a means to practical ends, if we look upon it as a servant of life rather than as a master—a master who becomes an unmerciful tyrant—the intellect possesses marvellous power and has a task of its own. Its task is not to penetrate into the meaning of reality, but to labor for the good of humanity by means of its working hypotheses. By means of these hypotheses it brings to the surface and makes available for the technician the materials which can be used for the welfare of the human organism and for the purpose of civilization. From this it is not to be inferred that the intellect plays only an insignificant part in the sphere of revelation. This error has cost humanity an appalling price. In religion it is poor policy to be miserly and suspicious toward the claims of the intelligence and weak and compliant toward self-satisfied obscurantism. There are many persons for whom religion means salvation and is a concern of the inner life platform for agitation or a field for self-seeking ambitions. It is no wonder that such persons seem unable to understand an interest in religion which is not bound up with worldly purposes. For such minds there is no such thing as an unmixed striving to attain knowledge of the truth in religion. There are, however, others for whom religion means salvation and is a concern of the inner life above all else. These ought never to forget that unwarranted claims of the intellect in religion cannot be answered by mere protests. The only effective answer is the discovery of the real sources and conditions of revelation in the life of the human spirit. This is gained only by an intense spiritual labor.

The task of the intellect in revelation is as important as it is extensive. First and last it constitutes an indispensable control. Without its weeding and trimming the plants of religion will grow wild. The criticism of the understanding is essential. Else zeal will degenerate into fanaticism, imagination into superstition, authority into clericalism and literalism. Furthermore, the intellect is needed to analyze and systematize the materials of religious conceptions and to investigate their history. Religion cannot stop with merely isolated facts and experiences. It must needs seek continuity and unity. Religion does not content itself with unquestioning acceptance of that which is handed down in the scriptural tradition. Religion seeks to grasp the history of revelation in its concrete reality and renews itself in contact with this concrete reality. Many of the great religious personalities have been famous thinkers, logicians, critics, scientists, and scholars. We have but to name Origen, Augustine, Thomas Aquinas, Wycliffe, Calvin, Pascal, Schleiermacher, Kierkegaard, Newman, Harnack, Al Ghazali, Nagarjuna, Sankara.

Error and confusion result, however, when the role of intellect is changed from that of control to that of source of knowledge. Its role as controlling, bringing order, criticizing, systematizing, is a restricted one, but is a great and indispensable one. We must not change it to one of being a source of knowledge, of being a real revelation. It is true that even in primitive religion the intellectual search for the ultimate cause seems to lie behind the conception of the All-Father. Natural religion, so-called, rests on the supposition that the understanding must conclude from the nature of the universe the existence of God. But even if this could be done, which I doubt, there would be no real religion until other elements are added.

To human reason we may concede a part greater or less, to play in the knowledge of God. There is found today and there has been found in the past in theological and ecclesiastical thought a view which holds that a normal person, using his understanding, by observing the workings of natural law and the order of the world, must necessarily by the compulsion of logic arrive at the conclusion that there is a Creator and that he is at work in the world. We know that Aristotle had this confidence in the powers of the intellect. After him we find it in the Roman theology developed under his influence, and especially in the great Thomas Aquinas of the Middle Ages. We find it later in evangelical thought, in the theologians of deism and of the Enlightenment. The Pope has now made Thomas Aquinas the normative theologian of the Roman church. It now belongs to Roman Catholic orthodoxy, as a Roman Catholic theologian has succinctly phrased it, to hold the first and second articles of the creed, not as affirmations of faith but as conclusions of the reason. Plato, Augustine, Occam, Luther, with modern evangelical theology, assign a far more modest role to the human understanding. According to their view faith and the religious experience and revelation are of far greater importance in attaining certainty of God and his works.

All knowledge includes an element of will. The interest, and consequently the desire of an inquirer, is directed toward the object of knowledge. When we examine an object and desire to know it, this means that, in a certain degree, we wish to possess it spiritually. This quality, which inheres more or less in all knowledge, is given an incomparably greater importance in that kind of knowledge which we call religious faith. Faith lays hold of God and holds to God, or rather, opens the way for the will and work of God and receives the love of God revealed in Jesus Christ. Faith is thus not a lesser degree of knowledge, as if, for example, one would say, I believe that the forests of northern Sweden are more beautiful than others, but I do not know whether they are. Rather, faith differs from other knowledge in its object. Faith is knowledge of the spiritual world. It differs from other knowledge in that it does not proceed from sense perceptions. Perhaps we here can apply the Hindu psychology with its doctrine of an inner sense, *Manas*, which perceives spiritual reality. Some have attempted to differentiate between the knowledge of faith and the knowledge of the understanding by making the former an interested knowledge constituting a value judgment, while the latter is an uninterested objective knowledge, an existential judgment. But this difference, as has been pointed out, is relative; the transition from one to the other is imperceptible. An element of value is found in all knowledge, and the object of faith possesses objectivity in fully as great degree as does that of knowledge based on the sense perceptions. If a comparison is to be made, it can be said that faith possesses a more certain assurance of its object than does other knowledge. For other knowledge does not possess such an all-devouring interest in its object. We could quote, in this connection, passages from Bhakti in Hinduism and Mahayana. Within the Christian church no one has more powerfully expressed the character of faith as certainty than has Martin Luther. He says of faith: "Faith receives the forgiveness of sins and makes us righteous and alive." "When the soul holds fast to the promises of God it cannot doubt that he is true, righteous, wise, and that he will act and order and care for all things in the best way. Is not such a soul, by reason of its faith, in everything most obedient to God?" Faith is more than simply a surmise or a thought. "If your conception of faith is that it is only thinking about God, then this thought can, as little as the garb of a monk, give you eternal life." Faith must consequently have its influence on the whole personality. "Faith is a certain and vital trust in the grace of God, so certain that one could die a thousand deaths on it. And this trust and knowledge of God's grace makes a man bold, joyful, and at peace with God and all created things. This the Holy Spirit works through faith. By faith a man becomes willing and disposed to do good to all without constraint, to serve and to suffer all things to please God who has shown so much grace toward him."

Melanchthon understood this correctly when he wrote in the

Apology of the Augsburg Confession, "Such a faith which has courage to trust in God, in life or in death, such a faith alone creates a Christian man."

We must consequently posit as the subject of faith, not the understanding, the human organ of knowledge only, but the whole spiritual being of man, which Pascal calls the heart. And if we wish to define more closely the powers of soul, the gifts or drives in man, which set faith in motion to seek God, we must necessarily come to consciousness of the infinite which we possess, consciousness of the spiritual reality which is beyond, which does not permit itself to be enclosed within measurable limits. And as another generating impulse to faith, we note the longing of man for perfection, his sense of lack and of sin and guilt, and his striving to attain to realization of the ideal. Revelation, that is to say, God and his works, cannot be grasped by man otherwise than by faith. Faith cannot be satisfied with anything less than God himself, as he has revealed himself.

The sources of revelation, or better still, its channels through which it comes to meet faith on the part of man, are two: the *consciousness of infinity* and the *urge to the ideal*. In one sense religion and revelation are universal, for they are found in some measure in all human beings. But in another sense they are particular. They are found only in individuals in whom the consciousness of infinity and the longing for the ideal have come to such definite form and found such clear content that they have been able to satisfy and gather about them numbers of those in humankind who hunger after salvation.

II

An obscure passage in the Book of Ecclesiastes seems to mean that "God has put eternity into the heart of man."[2] Whether this is the correct interpretation of the passage or not, it is nevertheless

[2] [Eccl. 3:11 (RSV).]

true. Many modern thinkers, as for example, C. P. Tiele, Louis Pasteur, F. von Hügel, would go so far as to make the consciousness of infinity the very basis of religion in man. There is found in man a perception which cannot be explained by what the eyes see and the ears hear. And perhaps Pasteur is right when he believes that the perception of the infinite is the most certain of all human perceptions. It introduces the soul into a higher world than the material, where the soul can breathe more deeply and freely. The heroes of the religion of infinity have won an eternally abiding home for thousands and thousands of noble and devoted souls. No one can read their writings without feeling that this infinite world, so distant from our outward world, possesses a reality, a power, a fascination. There is found a redemption and a refuge for the human spirit. In two instances in history the perception of the infinite world has brought forth types of religion which have gained significance in world history. To be sure they have not lacked ethical elements, the passion to realize ideals of conduct, but the controlling power has been the sense of the infinite. Not always has this been pure and unmixed, but nevertheless it has been the dominant element. From India I would cite the name of Yajnavalkya, one of the great names of the Upanishads, as representative of an obscure beginning which developed into movements of vast influence with continuance in Brahmanic and Buddhistic doctrines of redemption. In the West Plotinus is the great systematizer and mystic of the consciousness of infinity. He is the perfecter of Orphism and Platonism and was himself more or less normative of the mystical currents in Christianity and in the Islam of Persia. The Aryan spirit has given the longing for infinity its greatest depth and widest range. If one is an enthusiast for an Aryan or an Indo-Germanic form of piety, undoubtedly the religion of infinity here offers its best claim to being true-born. I use the term consciousness of infinity because, in my opinion, the mystical has a point of contact in every human being. The fact that contemplation and ecstasy and the blessed experience of union with God characterize the life of comparatively few persons depends on certain psychical predispositions and experiences in life and also, in some measure, on particular training and preparation. I must include in this brief paragraph concerning consciousness of infinity my conviction that visions, contemplation, do convey to mystically gifted men and women a real perception of the being of God. We sometimes speak of a sixth sense with which the mystic perceives the true reality hidden behind the world of phenomena. Whatever explanation we may offer for such unusual and remarkable conditions of the soul's life, it must be held true that they are related to feelings and experiences which, in some measure, every person possesses who has been awakened to the existence of spiritual realities.

III

The urge to ideals of conduct, or conscience, is concerned with a different kind of contrast between man and God than is the consciousness of infinity. If I may thus express it, the difference is one more purely qualitative. The decisive thing here is not the distance of the finite from the Infinite, the difference between the lowliness of man and the exaltation of God, between the noisy unrest of life and the stillness and peace of the eternal world. It is rather the difference between that which *is*, with all its lack, its inadequacy, its sin, and that which *ought to be*, perfection, realization, holiness. The longing for the ideal is revealed in the disturbance that conscience feels over the breach of certain rules of conduct. But it is deepened and intensified so that it finally becomes a burning passion for righteousness and purity, which reaches far beyond every outward regulation. It grows into an unending craving and yearning for perfection, which reveals the intimate connection which exists between the consciousness of infinity and the impulse to the ideal. In this latter I wish to point out three stages which have been of great significance in the history of religion. First, there is the ideal in the form of rules and ordinances which express the ethical demands of God and of his nature. Second, there is the ideal (with also the conception of deity) found in the form of a human person, a saint, a hero, an avatar, an incarnation, above all, in Christ, whom one is compelled so far as possible to imitate. The customs of the Prophet and his immediate followers is made the object of imitation in Islam, and the imitation of Christ is the goal of St. Francis and of Roman Catholicism. Finally there is the stage on which there is present an ideal and a conception of God which cannot be expressed in rules or qualities of character, nor does it consist strictly in the life of a person to be imitated, but in the spirit, which flows from the person and work of Christ. The pursuit of the ideal is directed beyond all that which is human and seeks its footing in a transmundane, a divine goodness. At four junctures in the history of religions has the urge to ideals brought forth or liberated significant formations, not entirely apart from the consciousness of infinity but nevertheless predominating over it. In China there was Laotse, in Iran Zoroaster, in Greece Socrates, and in Israel Moses—perhaps even Abraham. One is impressed in each of these cases with a spirit which is different from that produced by the consciousness of infinity, as the channel through which the revelation of the being of God has broken through into humanity. Perhaps the difference comes to light most clearly through a comparison of Socrates and Plato. The former is characterized by his faithfulness to conscience and his confident trust in divine providence, the latter by his exalting yearning. Nowhere, however, does the ethical zeal of God burn away all other elements and interests in revelation as in Moses and those who followed him. The good news of Christ is a message of the divine authority, of infinite seriousness, and love.

My thesis is this: in these two, the consciousness of infinity and the urge to the ideal, the wellsprings of religion flow forth upon the earth out of the innermost depths of the divine being. God reveals himself to us. Faith receives this revelation. In both there is a movement from the merely subjective to the objective, from the religious structure of the mind to the faith which is called forth by revelation. We are all more or less musically gifted—or at least, we will suppose that such is the case. Something of the life of music lives in all of us. But when Bach and Beethoven arise they become for us, not merely two persons much more musically gifted than the rest of us, but, rather, they are revelations of music itself. In them the spirit of music comes forth to meet us. I am almost as certain that we reach in Bach, in principle, the highest point in music, and that Plotinus constitutes the perfection of the mysticism of infinity, as I am that Christ will never be surpassed nor even equalled in the history of divine revelation. Of course this can have no demonstration logically.

It is much the same in religion. We all possess the sense of infinity and the longing for righteousness. We need make no exceptions here, as in the case of music. We all possess some share of the religious life. We are none of us excluded from the life of the spirit, the Spirit of God. But in some individuals the Spirit of God breaks forth with such mighty power that they become for us the revealers of God. In them God comes to meet us. When we see them we see something of God—even though no one of them can, in the same sense with Jesus, say: "He that hath seen me hath seen the Father."[3] These mirror in their character something of the power and love of God. Luther held that each one of us was to be a Christ to other men.

We observe here a peculiar difference between the religion which preferably perceives the divine under the aspect of infinity and that in which the reality of conscience predominates. In three respects this difference emerges, in respect to personality, to history, and to authority. Other important differences must here be left to one side. In the very nature of things religion of infinity is indifferent toward personality and history. It flees from the concrete, from the complexity of this life and the chain of events, one

[3] [John 14:9.]

following upon another, to the all-embracing mystery of the eternal world. But that religion which is born of and is nurtured by the longing for the ideal must concentrate in the personal life. For in the personal life only can that eye in the human soul which is called the imperative ideal recognize God and his revelation. And if the being of God is something which can be surmised by us at least approximately and can be expressed in the symbols of ethical self-realization and life-generating, redeeming, forgiving love, then the great drama of the human race must bear traces of this. In other words, history must in some sense be the epic of the divine will. The religion of the compelling power of ideals must necessarily draw history and the personal life within the area of revelation and find in these the revelation of God—while, on the other hand, the consciousness of infinity may, I do not say *must*, but may, according to its nature, be indifferent to human history and its personalities.

In consequence the question of authority will assume, in some degree, a different form in each. I mean the question of that authority which is able to give to religion its bearing and its strength. We can see this within Christianity, when religion has risen up out of its age of childhood and can no longer content itself with an outward authority, the dictation of a hierarchy or of the letter, or of a church majority. Mysticism, influenced by Platonism and Neoplatonism, has, in such a crisis, preferably fled away to its own ethereal regions, hid in its esoteric truth, unconcerned about every authority, lost in its own visions. On the other hand, a St. Paul, an Augustine, a St. Birgitta, a Luther, a Pascal, a Bunyan, a Kierkegaard, have transferred the authority to the person of Christ and bound it to the glorified figure of Christ, of his faith, his heart and mind. It is clear that creative, revealing personalities must have as such a wholly different significance for the pursuit of ideals than for the longing for infinity.

Revelation signifies that God makes himself felt, that the divine shimmers through the earthly medium. I maintain that the eyes through which humanity views the divine are two, the longing for infinity and the urge to the ideal. Both are valuable, in normal cases they are joined. But at times it is the one and at times the other which determines the soul's conception of God. In its great personalities the longing for infinity exalts above all and reveals to us the divine world of reality far above the petty cares and the narrow limits of this world. But in order that this exaltation shall not dissolve the divine there must be added the passion for the ideal, the hunger and thirst after an immeasurable transformation and exaltation of life. This passion courageously thrusts itself forward and achieves the impossible, becomes certain of the reality of this other world, certain of God's own nature in its positive and overwhelming majesty and power.

Where? In nature, in the movements of the worlds, in the flow and development of life? Yes, but only dimly, doubtfully. In order to see it there, revelation must first have taken place and been appreciated within the more intimate area, in conscience and in history. No one has better expressed this than the Swedish hymn writer, J. O. Wallin.[4] Having sung of the power, wisdom, and majesty of God proclaimed by a thousand tongues in nature, he continues:

> But still, Thy heart I could not trace,
> Thy purpose hidden lay,
> A mite in endless realms of space,
> Adrift I sought my way.

> On Sinai dawned the light at last,
> On Tabor came full day.
> My soul saw clear, the darkness past,
> Thy law, Thy will revealed.

> Earth's anguish gained a meaning clear,
> In Heav'n's revealing light;
> Celestial voices sang their cheer,
> Heard deep in human hearts.

[4] [J. O. Wallin (1779-1839) was a gifted poet and churchman who made a large contribution to Swedish hymnody. He also served as archbishop.]

This is the road which revelation has taken; this way it travels at all times. Nowhere else, however, is the certainty of the nature of God, as it is achieved by an intense passion to attain perfection, stronger than it is in the person of Jesus. In no other personality has this certainty in a more effective way penetrated the whole being. No one is therefore a revelation of God in the same sense as Jesus. In no one does the divine shine through as brightly as in him. It is not an arbitrary thing that we turn to him. One may ask, why just to him? The history of religion answers: there is for the resolve to attain the ideal no other choice. The effects of his life are such that they mark for him a central and unique place. Yet the development of his own personality and its influence is dependent essentially on the fact that he did not stand isolated. He is linked in the series of interpreters of the certainty of God, in a history which is more than typical, a history which as none other is freighted with revelation. These interpreters, the great figures of the passion for righteousness who lived before the day of Jesus, with those of our own day as well, and he himself above all, these persons and this history appear to us as a revelation in a unique sense. The motives, the powers, the conflicts have been in no other history by the actors themselves so clearly defined, lived through, and made use of in the same manner as by the prophets in the biblical history. The prophets and their followers have become martyrs for the faith in the God of history. I do not necessarily mean by this that any orthodoxy has condemned their faith as heresy. But their insistence on an ethical core in history has brought them into an attitude of tragic inner tension even if it has not led them to physical suffering and death. These martyrs of history bring their faith to victory.

Let no one at this point call attention to the infinitely small scale of the biblical history as compared with all that has transpired on our earth, and the infinitely small proportions of the whole of human history as compared with that of the universe. My answer to the former objection is that science must necessarily be empirical. It cannot concern itself with that which we beforehand hold probable.

Perhaps there ought to be found another history as enlightening concerning the will of God as is the biblical history. Perhaps there ought to be found revealers as remarkable as Christ. But in fact there are none. Science must take the actual, strange as it may be, and take it seriously. The answer to the latter objection of the insignificance of the human world in the vast expanse of space is that when we seek for principles, essence, and content, bulk does not overawe us. It is a purely relative thing whether I measure with the millionth of a millimeter or with a billion kilometers. In our experience reality is revealed in a more intensive and exalted form in human life than anywhere else in the universe.

Read, investigate, weigh carefully all that relates to this question! Some doubt may possibly arise as to which is to have the preference, consciousness of infinity or the urge to the ideal. There are those of our contemporaries who prefer the mysticism of infinity with the unity which it seeks. But if we value more the passion to attain the ideal, if we see in the impact of the divine will on life, in the purposefulness of existence a stronger power for salvation and a richer future blessing vouchsafed the soul and the human race than is offered in a religion which catches only a glimpse of the divine in a far-off, peaceful stillness, in refuge from the temporal and the historical, then there is no doubt that in the life of Christ and in the history in which that life is set, we have the revelation of God *par préférence* within humanity, enduring and not to be surpassed. In his life and in this history, if anywhere, the cold crust of the earthly life is broken through and the warming, glowing, consuming fire of the divine Spirit breaks forth, active ever as the Spirit of the risen Lord. Christ and the biblical history, however, do not become truly a revelation until the veil has been taken from our eyes and we are led to see the divine life, the will of God beneath all of existence. If we have put our whole being into this undertaking, if we have sounded the depths through our own effort and meditation, we shall be conscious of this divine life and will in our own inner life. We shall also see it revealed in that human history in which we ourselves stand fighting and suffering. It shall be revealed to us in the phenomena of nature, in the development of life below the level of the human, perhaps also in the changes and the laws of inorganic nature.

How can the coherence, in which science believes and which it finds present in all that exists and all that happens, how can this become a revelation to us, a testimony to the living God, to the reality of the divine will? Nearest at hand lies the expedient of translating the causal connection into purpose. The view is lifted to the future. That which happens is not simply the result of causes, but also points to an end. For example, I am walking aimlessly through a crowd, partly pushed on by those behind me, partly myself seeking a way out into the open. Just then I meet a person, and that meeting becomes decisive for my life. This event I necessarily ascribe to a purposeful guidance, an end. Another example. Concurring events bring me into a situation which I bitterly lament. Years later I bless it as something which served a purpose unknown at the time. Again, science depicts the history of Israel merely as causal continuity leading up to the appearance of Jesus. Faith sees in this history a preparation for the great goal, Christ. Again, science studies the laws of heredity. If we only knew all the factors —which is impossible—we could, out of the many genealogies, derive that combination which resulted in the spiritual endowment of Gustavus Vasa, the founder of the modern Swedish state. It is clear to us that he was the man who was predetermined and equipped for his task.

Such transitions from causality to teleology have their validity within certain limits. But objections arise against viewing the problem of revelation as solved by permitting those generalizations, which we call the laws of nature, to become valid as the will of God. The continuity of reality concealed from us is one thing; our generalizations and the "laws of nature" are another.

1. We must be on our guard against a teleological explanation in the style of the meditations of the cat on the fact that birds have

wings, which of course deprives the hungry cat of her food, perhaps at the very instant when her claws are about to grasp it. This causes vexation of spirit for the cat. She finds the world order unjust but solves the difficulty by nourishing the hope of a millennium, when birds will no longer have wings. This parable comes to my mind, a reminiscence from a book by Östrup on cats, whenever I hear pious teleological reasonings, which drag the secrets of the soul with its diabolical temptations and its comforting celestial visions of struggling faith down to the level of a shabby utilitarianism.

2. Still more serious is another difficulty. Causality sometimes turns out to be the most cruel lack of purpose. Shall we then be comforted by the hope that this also shall at last receive a satisfactory explanation in a higher light? This hope does not satisfy. Revelation is not to be found in a translation of causal continuity nor in a new insight into its meaning. Revelation is *a struggle against resisting forces.* Within all areas of life we discover plainly the contrast between the dull, dead thing, which hinders and chokes progress and itself falls prey to dissolution, and that vital power, which is forever striving forward, always nearly overcome but yet always unwearied and conquering. On the higher levels this contrast is acute. There is something in that which happens both within and without the human world which drags down and hinders. God's continuing creation, an ever continuing creation, is also a continuing struggle. I can see what a contradiction this means for the search after a unified world view. I am also fully conscious of the imperfections in the attempt of our thought to comprehend and express the ways of reality and the life of God. It is clearer than ever to me that dualism—not an absolute dualism, but one with hope and certainty of the attainment of unity—more accurately than monism reproduces reality the more deeply we penetrate into its very life. Anyone who has been rocked to sleep in monism has never felt "the depths of satan." I do not begrudge him his escape. But he cannot claim the right to speak as an interpreter of life.

Rather than a translation of causality into teleology, I would commend another view. We are confronted by two different planes, the plane of science and the plane of revelation. In both we are concerned in some sense with reality. In science it is, however, in a very abstract way. That is to say, our knowledge gathers up out of reality that which can be arranged within the causal continuity and such as constitutes the condition necessary for the adaptation of nature to our purposes. Of course this scientific view of the totality with its hypotheses stands in an intimate relation with reality. The two planes do not lack connection the one with the other. But the task of science is not simply theoretical, not simply to know, but to rule. The plane of revelation is different. Here we penetrate deeper than we are able to do with the intellect alone. Here we must throw ourselves, for life or death, into a wrestling with reality itself. We discover that we certainly are not the conquerors. If we are to experience the restoring power we must realize that we are completely defeated. If we are to find a revelation we must seek for and we must discover something solid on which to build. It is not a question of an intellectual game, nor of an investigation which possesses only practical significance and whose criterion of truth is practical utility. On the contrary, we seek to penetrate into and to catch the message of reality itself. The truth is that God himself presses in upon us.

We can, as I have shown in a number of examples, superimpose the plane of science upon the plane of revelation and seek to express the matter thus: God works through the laws of nature. But essentially the two views serve different purposes. The so-called laws of nature do not give us the essence of reality. No critical scientist believes that reality consists of the ether or the atoms, but we know well, professional scientists and others, that God is the true reality.

Certainty of the living God we gain, as did the prophets and the apostles, by an experience of communion with the life of God. The more wholeheartedly we can devote ourselves to reality, that is, to the demands which life makes on us to repent and to obey, either in fiery efforts or in quiet self-dedication and rest, the more certain are we to gain and to retain the conviction that God does exist and that he is an unfathomable goodness, fighting his way through and that he is able to carry us through. If we are strictly conscientious and exacting we must admit that we are not able to perceive much of the revelation of God. In every case, this is our fault, not God's. Still, we know that we have met him in our life, we are conscious as we look back upon life, of his guidance. History unveils for us at times God's way of dealing. In a situation which appears without comfort or help there shines through it all a sense of the purpose of God—shall we dare to lay hold on it and believe in it? We must believe, in spite of all! We must hope against all hope! If the mere event as a dead thing rises up before us and obscures our view of revelation, we must go to the Bible. There heaven is open and its light penetrates through the grey mists and fearful darkness of our life.

Only as we pray and labor are we able to hold fast the revelation. The mystic speaks of a purification, a *via purgativa*, which constitutes the first rung of the ladder to heaven upon which he seeks to reach the divine life. To this purification belongs the ethical life of man and its development. In reality the connection between the moral life of man and his communion with God is closer than this. Only as active champions for the eternal goodness in ourselves and others do we create within us that attitude in which we can truly commune with God. That man has little or no need of questioning concerning the existence and work of God who prays and labors with soul and body in the power of his prayer, "If any man willeth to do his will, he shall know of the teaching, whether it be of God, or whether I speak of myself."[5] No one can possibly doubt the existence of that One, with whom he communes earnestly and with greater interchange than with any human being. "In him we live and move and have our being."[6] He is our life.

[5] [John 7:17.]
[6] [Acts 17:28.]

3

CONTINUED REVELATION

I

In certain of the later writings of the Old Testament and in Judaism, piety no longer discerns the activity of God in the historical events and personalities of the present. It is more likely to be found in the wise and magnificent order of nature. In history it is found only in the ancient miracles of revelation. By reason of the place which Christ was given in the Christian's communion with God, Christianity finds itself in a different situation regarding faith in revelation. A certain likeness is found, however, *mutatis mutandis*, between the Judaism which retained the certainty of revelation only in that which happened long ago, and the average Protestant conception, according to which the revelation of God is a finished product of antiquity and written down in its entirety in the Holy Book.

"And God said unto Moses." So ran the lesson in Bible history a boy was reading aloud as he studied. His younger, more rationalistically inclined brother interrupted him with the words: "But God cannot speak to human beings in that manner." The school boy knew the right answer: "Hush, he could in those days."

Into this view there is woven a bit of inalienable Christian conviction. Revelation is a thing at hand, completed once for all in Jesus Christ and since his day needs not to be remade or improved. John records the words of Jesus concerning the Spirit: "He shall take of mine, and shall declare it unto you."[1] Christ, who suffered

[1] [John 16:14.]

under Pontius Pilate, the Christ of history, in the light of faith is valid for all time. The history, which is related in the Bible, constitutes the revelation of God in a fuller, richer, weightier sense than that of any other history. The unique revelatory quality of the history recorded in the Bible appears impossible and unbelievable to a priori reasoning, but receives to a certain extent a surprising confirmation in the comparative study of religions, when this science has had sufficient time to find its bearings in the confusing abundance of its material.[2] For history is not made according to the laws of logic. What one finds there may be quite absurd, indeed, one would say beforehand, that it is unthinkable. But still, it has happened. It is material for scientific investigation, which must in this case, as always, in order to reach genuine results, take its position beneath its object of investigation, listening, absorbing, interpreting; not above its object in an attitude of domination. In the history of religion there is revealed a supernatural life, but not always what human thought might esteem just and correct. As we have sought to show earlier in this book, the actual appearance of the history of religion agrees with the words of St. Paul about a general revelation, within which we can discern a special revelation. Or, to use terms which do not have any metaphysical import, within the religion of the race appear certain phenomena, which in a special sense deserve the name revealed religion. To show, however, how impossible it is to hold that there is in truth such a divine revelation and at the same time to hold that it is concluded for all time in Christ and the Bible, it is necessary only to combine two questions: "Does God continue to reveal himself to humanity?" and: "Has God ever revealed himself to humanity?" The latter question lies threateningly behind the former and shows how impossible it is to maintain that there is a true revelation unless we assume that it continues in the present time. How can we convince a man who does not believe that there is a divine influence, and for

[2] Cf. chap. 2, and also my article, "Communion with Deity," in Hasting's *Encyclopedia of Religion and Ethics*.

whom there exists no living God that a God really exists who at one time revealed himself to man, if God does not now reveal himself to that man as living and redeeming him? And yet there are Christians who believe in God, not simply as a law or principle, a great, all-penetrating mystery, but as a will and as love which has made itself known to man, and yet maintain that revelation closed with Christ and the Bible. The following discussion is therefore intended as a contribution toward the further development of the Christian idea of revelation. I call attention to a continuing divine self-impartation, which manifests itself as a creating power and a redeeming will. Most clearly this is shown in three areas of life, in nature, in history, and in the moral life. These may be further defined by three phenomena: 1) genius as a phase of nature, 2) the continuity and purposiveness of history, 3) the regeneration of the individual and the formation of character. If this continued revelation takes place within Christendom it marks the continued action of Christ. Belief in and experience of his living power is the identifying characteristic common to all Christianity.

The theologians of Pius X and Professor Wilhelm Herrmann were agreed upon one point: God has revealed himself in Jesus Christ. But at once their ways parted. In more recent evangelical thought there has emerged a conception of revelation which because of its concentration assumes a position as solid as rock and as hard as diamond. It is the conception that revelation does not consist in any individual events or any statements or writings. It consists in the inner life of Christ in relation to the Father and in his love, so divinely fixed and powerful. If, however, one has met God in Christ, one can no longer isolate Christ. The man who says: "God is revealed in Christ," at the same time says: "God is revealed in nature." The man who says: "God is revealed in Christ," cannot escape saying: "God is revealed in history."

The ancient church used the term "nature" concerning Christ. However anxious the theology of our time may be to observe and to preserve continuity with that which the church at that time pronounced as a postulate of faith—two natures, one divine, the other human—it must nevertheless today take other aspects of the matter for its investigation and express the being of the Savior in other terms. Do we consider the divine to be a nature? Is there a nature which is specifically super-animal or human? What we call nature, is it really nature conceived in the ancient manner as substance? In recent times another distinction has been made as to the person of Christ. Modern theology draws a line between nature and character, between that in Jesus which was given, inherited, "natural," just as in any human being, and that which was the product of his will, his self-discipline, that is, his ethical personality, his character, the seriousness and purity of love and righteousness in him, that which we call the ethical and spiritual life in any human being. Under the influence of its heritage from pietism and rationalism, modern theology has viewed the saving power of Christ as residing in his ethical perfection and mighty love. Such a view means indeed an advance in the apprehension of Christ and of revelation. But is it satisfactory? Let us ask from a purely empirical and historical standpoint: "What elements in the person of Christ constitute his unparalleled religious significance, according to the testimony of history?" I do not now refer to the uniqueness of the historical situation or to other religio-historical circumstances, concerning which we shall have occasion to speak in another paragraph in this chapter. The answer is, naturally, his spiritual and moral greatness, the intense seriousness of his will, his divinely passionate mercy, his powerful intuition of personal truth. Certainly, these are the most important elements.

But can we stop with these? Take any foundation-laying personality, prophet or great saintly figure that you will, can his influence be explained solely by his ethical glory and his supreme goodness? No indeed. Behind him lies nature—in his mighty endowments. He has not created himself. From whence has he come? In a sermon written in 1544 Luther asks: "St. Peter, St. Paul, Augustine, Ambrose, John Huss, I myself, Dr. Martinus, from

whence have all these come?" Had he been ever so holy and determined, could Pascal have accomplished what he did or attained to
the place he holds in the kingdom of God if he had not been born
into this world with the exquisite and powerful gifts we all admire
in him? And these were his without any of his own doing. In an
immensely greater degree this holds true of Christ. My objection is
that we seek to understand the deity of Christ only on the basis of
his truth, his holiness and love, without taking into account the treasures of his incomparable gifts, which lay hidden already in the
womb of Mary—that is, without reckoning with the revelation of
God in nature and through nature. That Jesus became the Savior of
the world was due, not only to his moral greatness but, in the first
place, to the mystery of the endowment which was his from birth,
to the incarnation. "The word became flesh." The revelation is
given, not alone in the holiness of Christ, but also in the miracle of
his nature, of his human blood. One could add that the close union
between natural gifts and ethical power often puts to a severe test
our longing to see righteousness established in the world order. To
find anything like an illuminating comparison or point of contact
for the interpretation of the person of Christ, it is clear that we
must turn to the extraordinary personalities in history. Any view of
the deity of Christ which cuts off every connection with these is as
much contrary to dogma as to the gospel.

The emergence of *genius* is in its way a constant demonstration
of the truth that the essence of reality is creation, the eternal creation of something new, not a dead connection of cause and effect.
Or, in other words, the inner compulsion which lies behind that
which is visible to our eyes and audible to our ears is a necessary
urgency to create, to generate, to save, to make alive, to bring forth
something new out of the hidden treasures of being. It is not a
mechanical necessity, which simply administers and in new ways
combines that which is already at hand. In the phenomenon of
genius there breaks forth a mighty wave of creative power. It is
clear to us that the genesis of genius follows determined laws.

Many genealogies lie behind the child, in whose unborn body lie slumbering wondrous treasures. Inheritance, dangerous inheritance, good inheritance, weak inheritance, through thousands of changes of heredity in its forebears produces differing results. A combination and a reciprocal influence come from the talents of father and mother, but not from them only, but also from earlier inheritances. The parents pass these on from the generations before them in a mysterious way to the individual or individuals, who after them take over the hidden possibility for good or for evil. This the parents often do without having themselves benefited from their values or suffered from their weight. The endowment of genius itself usually breaks forth to all appearance as suddenly and as much unmediated as the biological phenomenon, which since de Vries has been called mutation, a term which aims to express the inexplicable in the affair. In lower organisms, in plants and the lower orders of animals, remarkably keen analyses have been made of the conditions of heredity. Certainly there are hidden laws of heredity, which can be in part discovered by scientific investigation. Innumerable facts and details in previous generations must be taken into account in seeking an explanation of the suddenness and mysteriousness with which genius emerges before men's eyes. No mere process of addition of lofty and refined qualities will yield such a result. The riddle of generation and heredity is more complex than any sum in addition. We shall never be able fully to analyze the sources of a creative spirit and the constitutive elements in it. But we believe and know in all of higher culture that there is no such thing as chance, nothing merely happens, there is no break in the chain of real connection, although human eyes cannot penetrate the series of causes and effects.

The Christian faith and the synthetic view of life and history also know something more. They know that God works in the complex connections of the generations and that the right man is found at hand to perform his work when he is needed. Alas, it seems necessary again to emphasize that our line of thought is not concerned with the manner in which genius suddenly emerges. Its sudden, puzzling character is due to our imperfect analysis of the sequence of the generations. We are here concerned with the character of genius itself, with the results, not the method. In a measure it is true of every human being that it possesses in its being something original and unique, which is not fully like any other. Geijer has given us a word which is not only one of the most comforting that have been spoken, but also one of the truest. He says that there does not exist a person who cannot do some one thing better than anyone else. In creative genius, however, the new and the unique is revealed more clearly than in others. The phenomenon of creative spirits make us surmise that life in its reality is a continuing creation, not simply an administration.

Genius pursues one way of working, whatever may be the material with which it works. This material may be the hearts of men, states, armies, tones, colors, figures, fabrics, words. Language has with sure instinct fixed on the word which describes what is done with this material. It is creation. Something new emerges, something original, not found before. It is not always easy to determine wherein the new thing consists. But the fact that it is new distinguishes the work of genius from that of the merely talented. We can see this distinction more clearly if we but note the fact that the work of talent, be it ever so remarkable, but still merely talent, consists in a skillful reproduction according to rules and patterns. The work of genius, however, gives rise to new rules, which analysis afterwards discovers. *Creation* comes first, in revelation, in beauty of character, in social structure, in the work of art. Afterwards comes *doctrine,* in theology, in ethics, in theory of government, in theory of art. Exactly as in nature, the world of God's material creation; first flowers, then botany. Genius emerges as an essential element in the continuing creation of the Almighty. Genius is often also conscious of participation in a miracle. Plato knew that those who were inspired uttered the meaning of which they themselves were unable to grasp. Harald Hjärne has said:

"Not all seers are able to interpret their own visions." History verifies this observation. God alone knows the interpretation. Coming generations never tire of seeking to penetrate more and more deeply into the works of genius and of drawing from them constantly new instruction and edification. There is for us professors a very healthy warning in the paradox that great men are always right even when they contradict one another.

Having said this, however, the entire meaning of the creative work of genius has scarcely even been hinted at. Genius possesses another aspect even more wonderful, to which attention is seldom called. Perhaps I may call this the organic connection between the continuing creation of God and the work of men of genius. *Men of genius are the appointed interpreters of God's creation.* Existence is difficult to interpret and easily appears meaningless, bitterly meaningless. Through their powers of penetration, through their personalities and their creations, men of genius aid us to see or to surmise a meaning in life. This they do, not merely as thinkers. No, not primarily as thinkers, but as doers, as heroes, martyrs, prophets, saints, as artists, inventors, composers, poets. Their unique endowment reveals thus a mysterious connection with creation itself. Let me illustrate with a very humble example. We say, perhaps with a bit of merry snobbishness: "This sunset is like a picture of this or that painter." And it is really so, for before him and without him no one ever saw the same glory and the same colors. Why is it that for thousands of years Europeans saw no beauty in a wild mountain landscape? It is only in the last one hundred and fifty years that men have seen it. Luther journeyed through Switzerland twice without seeing the Alps, and yet he had ordinarily keen eyes to see the beauty of nature. Rousseau and Romanticism taught the Western world the glory of the Alps. In China and Japan the beauty of the snow-capped mountains had been appreciated far earlier. But in both cases it was genius which revealed the matter, that is, interpreted God's creation. Genius points the way; afterwards it is as easy as Columbus' egg. Something similar is revealed in the far more important areas of life. As regards poetic and artistic genius the matter has been expressed by Geijer[3] in the following words: "Humanity has a hard and laborious way to traverse. Goals and rules constitute what we call the divine order. His plan God has hidden in his divine wisdom, but he has given it to his most beloved creatures to study as a school exercise, a problem to meditate upon and to solve. This task is now proceeding in a strange and fragmentary manner, as it appears to our eyes, and there would be faint hope of the task's ever being successfully finished were it not for the fact that the Schoolmaster has his hand in the matter. The thought is for us awe-inspiring that the very idea of order would be lost if it could be proved only by the outward reality. Faith certainly fixes its eye on the goal, but sees only in part. It discerns perhaps no more than the golden cross which surmounts the spire of the temple. Science searches for the ground plans, but its work is also fragmentary. Therefore God has placed along this long and toilsome road of humanity's progress persons who possess the unique ability to bring forth for our reflection, out of their own inner life, in different ways and with different materials—words, sounds, colors, proportions—*pictures* which shine with the light of God's order. Such a light of glory we call beauty, and it refreshes the heart of man."

Geijer's words show us how the *interpreter* of creation and the *instrument* of creation coincide with each other. Still more clear does this connection become when we come to the men of genius in history. No genius of the higher order has ever been able to content himself with finding the universe and life meaningless, and halted in materialism. In history we find a line of men of genius who have in wider or narrower spheres created a meaning for life, when life seemed ready to dissolve in egoistic narrowmindedness and inert disintegration. Men of genius transform the situation. Life, a moment ago as empty as an empty sack or as sluggish as a full sack, awakens anew under their touch, becomes manly and alert.

[3] [Cf. *supra*, p. 79, footnote 42.]

Powers undreamed of—ah, were there really such powers in ordinary human beings!—gather and set themselves to the accomplishment of superhuman tasks. We know this from the history of nations. How was not all of Denmark stirred by Absalon, as later by the great Margaret! How did life in France not receive new strength and new will through Jeanne d'Arc or the Great Revolution—may the great little virgin forgive me for classifying them together! The same thing happened in England under Elizabeth and again under Cromwell; in Sweden under Gustavus Vasa and Gustavus Adolphus; in Russia through Peter the Great; in the United States through Washington; in Germany through Bismarck. The seriousness and spiritual power in these personalities filled their epoch with meaning and sacrifice. At times we long for the return of those days to lift us out of the musty and muddy days of the present. As Carlyle writes in the introduction to the *Letters of Cromwell*: "The ancient Reign of God, for which all true men have always striven in their several dialects and modes, giving place to the modern reign of No-God, whom men call Devil—this in its multitudinous meanings and results is a sight to create reflection in the earnest man." His desire that there should be found a history of all heroisms means, for me, that there should be found a history of the continued revelation of God. The important thing for us is that our eyes be opened to see the heroisms of our own day, and not the least, those which are demanded for the problems which lie before us in the present.

More widely and more profoundly than the men of political life go the heroes of religion. They have fought and won—no, I should not say won—they have received on their knees a new certainty of the meaning of the ways of God. They fought for their cause and for their time, but the gain has become ours. God was with them and his Spirit operates through them still.

Melanchthon, in a letter written in 1537, describes Luther as a God-sent prophet. It is not surprising that the sorrow at Luther's death took such forceful expression. Dr. Jonas said in his funeral sermon at Eisleben that previously God's great men and prophets had lived when times were at their worst, and that when they passed away terrible judgments always followed. Melanchthon gave utterance in his lectures to the following words: "The doctrine of the forgiveness of sins and of the faith in the Son of God has not been discovered by the subtlety of the human mind. It has come by revelation from God through this man [Luther] whom he raised up." In his Latin funeral sermon he points out that God's presence in the church is attested by the Lord's chosen servants, who are the choicest flower of humanity. Bugenhagen spoke of Luther's high office as apostle and prophet and called to mind the prophecy of John Huss. According to Dürer, Luther was regarded by his century as a *gottgeistig* man, a God-inspired man, foretold in the Bible and by the prophets of the Middle Ages. Johann Klajus from Herzberg wrote: "Just as the Holy Spirit spoke pure Hebrew through Moses and the prophets, and pure Greek through the apostles, so has he spoken good German through his chosen servant Luther." A much more authoritative testimony is given by the *Formula of Concord*, which not only calls Luther "the chief framer of the Confession of Augsburg" but also says that "this highly enlightened man (in the Latin text, 'this hero endowed with the Holy Spirit's unique and highest gifts'), saw in the Spirit what should happen after his death."[4] Older Lutheran theologians reserve for Luther in their dogmatics a special locus, which we must regard as an attempt to justify the continuance of revelation. John Gerhard, the greatest of the Lutheran scholastics, quotes many times the call of Luther, especially in his defense against the papal theologians. He considered the refutation of the arguments against the legitimacy and the divine plan in the raising up of Luther as a part of the justification of the evangelical denominations as being themselves the true Catholic church.[5] At the jubilee of 1617, Gerhard devoted a dispu-

[4] [*Formula of Concord*, Solid Declaration, VII, 28, in Tappert (ed.), *The Book of Concord*, p. 574.]

[5] Notice the title of Johann Gerhard's *Confessio catholica, in qua doctrina catholica et evangelica, quam ecclesiae Augustanae confessioni addictae profitentur, ex Romano-catholicorum scriptorum suffragiis confirmatur* (1634-37).

tation to the call of Luther. In his dogmatics he touches on the matter many times and in chapter 26 it is discussed in a special section. In the chapter touching the last judgment, he denies the papal contention that Luther was a false prophet because he had said that the judgment was soon to come.[6] In the chapter concerning the church[7] the double assertion of Lutheran dogmatics, that Luther's call was both *ordinaria* and *extraordinaria,* is especially defended against Cardinal Bellarmine. The proofs of the former were the fact that Luther had received in a regular manner the call and the ordination to the office of priest in 1507, the validity of which was not impaired by the irregularity of the ordaining bishop; furthermore, there was his degree of Doctor of Theology, with the oath which made it his duty not to proclaim heretical doctrines, and also the legal call to the professorship in Wittenberg University in 1507. As for his extraordinary call, Bellarmine held that it must be proved by miracle. Gerhard asks if it is not a miracle that a man without force of arms, with only the force of the Word and weapons of the unarmed, was able to break the supreme power in the world. For

> Rome has dominated the world but got the pope as Lord,
> The city used force, the pope used fraud.
> Greater than both is Luther, because he, for city and world,
> Became a teacher true, by his pen alone.[8]

As regards Luther's commission to reform the church and to reveal Anti-Christ, this consisted, according to Gerhard, in something more than the ordinary call to the priesthood. "Although he was not called immediately of God as were the prophets and the apostles, and although he did not speak with the

---

[6] *Loci theologici* (8 vols.; Jena, 1615-23), XXXI, 84. Cf below pp. 132 f.
[7] *Loci theologici,* XXV, 200.
[8] *Roma orbem domuit, sed Romam Papa subegit,*
Viribus illa suis, fraudibus iste suis.
Quantum isto major Lutherus major et illa.
Orbem urbemque uno qui docuit calamo.

immediate inspiration of the Holy Spirit as they did (because of this some deny that Luther's call was extraordinary, that is, immediate), it cannot be denied that there was something extraordinary and unique in this work of reformation and the revealing of Anti-Christ." This is proved also by prophecies in the Bible and by Luther's equipment, his powers of soul, success, etc. In chapter 26, *De ministerio ecclesiastico*, a whole section (viii) is devoted to the subject "Concerning the Call of the Blessed Luther" (*De vocatione Beati Lutheri*), and along the line given above the argument is carried out in detail.

It was not difficult for the theologians to find in the writings of Luther reference to his call to the gospel ministry which he had received in regular order. It is well known what a support Luther, like many others after him, found in the public obligation thus laid upon him. "I have often said," he writes, "and say it still, that I would not take all the treasure in the world for my doctorate. For I should in truth be finally disheartened and despair in the difficult matter which rests upon me if I had begun it by stealth, or of my own will, without a divine call and command. But both God and man must now give me the testimony that I have begun it publicly in my office as doctor and preacher." Gerhard writes that just as the priests of Jerusalem attacked the regularity of John the Baptist and of Christ (John 1:25; Matt. 21:23), just so the papal clerics now do with Luther. As we shall see in the following pages, it is by no means difficult to find also in the mouth of Luther himself very strong words about the extraordinary endowment and the task with which God had entrusted him.

But such expressions, with the exception of the prophecy of Huss, which Luther applied to himself, are not used by John Gerhard. Quenstedt expressly states that Luther never anywhere based his authority on any immediate and extraordinary call.[9] He is right in this. Luther was anxious, as were also the systematic theologians

---

[9] *Theologia didacti-polemica, sive systema theologicum* (Wittenberg, 1691), XII, esp. 3.

who followed him, to validate the official regularity and continuity in his action. This did not, however, affect the clear certainty which he also had that he was an extraordinary instrument of God. It is easy to understand that the Lutheran theologians, in their defense and polemic against the papal party, would not make use of such sayings, valuable though they may be for our understanding of Luther, because his enemies then, even as now, interpreted them as being the utterance of an ungodly, even a diabolical arrogance. Gerhard and the dogmaticians before and after him seek proof of "the extraordinary, even unparalleled element, which although it does not completely coincide with the immediate and entirely unique call of the apostles," still rises above the ordinary priestly call. They seek this proof preferably—almost exclusively—in known facts, only exceptionally in any strong words of Luther about himself. Aegidius Hunnius, characterized by contemporaries as "one of the chief of those theologians who wish to be called Lutheran," fixed upon a term by which to designate the extraordinary element in the call of Luther, a term earlier used about him,[10] and which Gerhard and others adopted as expressing a position midway between the apostles and other servants of the church. Luther's call is said to be "heroic" (*heroica*).

Gerhard brings forward six proofs or series of proofs: 1) predictions or prophecies in the Scriptures (Jer. 51:48; Dan. 11:44; Mal. 4:5; II Thess. 2:9; Rev. 14:6), and the prophecy of Huss about the rise of Luther; 2) the outstanding and uncommon gifts of Luther, "with which God richly and mercifully endowed his instrument for the battle against the kingdom of Anti-Christ, such as his rare learning, great skill in languages, keenness of judgment, an almost miraculous ability to translate the Scriptures, divine eloquence, a special power of the Spirit in almost every sentence"; 3) "Luther's heroic courage even in the greatest of dangers"; 4) his miraculous escape from treachery and violence; 5) his own predictions of coming events (here Gerhard refers to a special essay on Luther's

[10] *Disp. 10 in Augustanam Confessionem,* according to J. Gerhard.

predictions and to the locus about the church;[11] and 6) the remarkable progress of the evangelical preaching unaided by worldly
power, through the Word alone. Quenstedt discusses the same
argument in his stiffly scholastic *Systema theologicum* under the
question: "Was Luther's call to the teaching office in the church
legal and in conformity with the prevailing order?"[12] Among the
additional proofs, moreover, which he cites for an extraordinary
divine appointment he names the restoration of the doctrine of
"justification which gives life" and of "living words which flow out
of faith," and also the rich spiritual hymns and glowing, efficacious
prayers of Luther.

In a certain degree many of the true and great saints of Christendom reveal in their own favored spirits something of the character
of God himself. They visualize for us how the Father of our Lord
Jesus Christ lives and works even until now. But of no one, as far
as my knowledge and judgment go, is this true in higher degree
than of Martin Luther, whether one observes the originality and
prophetic meaning of his thoughts, or the freshness, the power and
richness of his personality as a testimony to the living presence of
God. He shared with Socrates, Christ, St. Paul, and the very greatest
—and, we might add, with some whom we may think under mere
illusion—a consciousness of his own importance. Already in 1521,
in a letter of January 25 to his elector, he called attention to the
claim that he had done everything for the salvation and blessedness
of Christendom and for the good of the German nation. In 1533
he wrote in the preface to his defense against the accusation of
Duke George that he incited to treason: "Such a boast and honor
have I by the grace of God that, whether the devil and all his creatures like it or not, since the days of the apostles no doctor or
writer, no theologian or jurist, has so gloriously defended, enlightened, and comforted the conscience of the laity as I have done,
through the special grace of God. This I know most certainly. For
not even St. Augustine and St. Ambrose, although they are the best

[11] Par. 300 should be par. 290.
[12] Chap. XII, qu. iii.

in this matter, are in these things equal to me. I boast of this with thanks and to the praise of God, and to the pain and chagrin of the devil and all my tyrants and enemies."[13] "Of the gifts of God one should boast," he writes in another place. A superficial judgment or prejudice sees in such words mere arrogance. But study the man thoroughly, observe his artless humility, and note his significance in the history of religion, in the history of the revelation of God. See him battling against the hell of anguish and despair, or, again, in trusting faith "exultingly rejoice that he has a merciful God and Father, yea, resolve with a fearless and unconquerable spirit to break his way through mountains of brass and all manner of opposition and declare that all flows with honey, milk and wine; no longer mortal, but living the life eternal."[14] No one can have penetrated deeply into the man without recognizing even in his boastful words the clear understanding such as favored men of God have had of their call, an insight which did not make them vain.

When men of genius wholeheartedly and consciously serve God they become saints. The doctrine of the saints lost its place in evangelical theology when the cult of saints was eliminated in the name of the gospel. I concede that the Roman church is so far right in its doctrine of the saints that the saints are those Christians who in an extraordinary way reveal the power of God. But divine power must not be conceived of in the primitive way, as revealed in unusual acts to be classed as miracles, which many would refer to suggestion. It must rather be conceived of as acting in accordance with a Christian conception of God.[15] The meaning of the word "saint" has been distorted in different ways. Some conceive of saints as objects of cult and reverence, as though they were something in themselves. Their own testimony is that they possess nothing of

[13] Erlangen edition 31, 236 [Weimar edition 38, 103].

[14] Cf. J. Gottschick, "Das Verhältnis von Diesseits und Jenseits im Christentum," *Zeitschrift für Theologie und Kirche,* IX (1899), 149.

[15] For the *Catechismus ex decreto concilii tridentini,* III, qu. 2, viii-xiv, saints are in reality objects of a cult, whose veneration and invocation must be regulated only so that the glory of God is not trespassed. For the meaning of *sanctus,* see H. Delehave in *Analecta Bollandiana,* sec. XXVIII, p. 145 ff. See also the essay on saints in my *När stunderna växla och skrida* (Saml. 2; Stockholm, 1910).

themselves of which they can boast, but all is of God. I can think of no more accurate description of the saints than this: saints are those who, in life, in spirit, and in deeds, clearly and unmistakably show us that God lives. Could I name saints who are living today? Or again some whose character and fellowship remain as real to us as when they were living in our circle and near us, although they have passed from the earthly scene? I do not think it necessary to cite any names. Those of us who use a little thought will find many who are truly saints.

II

A place of honor is due those great figures of religion who have put their soul into the task of serving and seeing the will of God in *history.* I purposely use the order, *serve and see.* For in the kingdom of God no one can see so long as he remains merely a spectator. Those only who serve the will of God freely and sacrificially can see the will of God. In other affairs the order may well be that one should first look into a matter and understand it before one enters upon it. In the kingdom of God the opposite is true. Here we enter upon *history* as the second area of the continuing revelation of God. We must now turn to those who have been the first to see in history a real disclosure of God, namely, Moses and the prophets, and in some measure also the prophet of Iran, Zoroaster. Others before them have interpreted history as a mere sequence of events in the past and present. History, conceived of as purposing something higher than all merely human calculations and combinations of power,[16] leading on to the complete victory of God, to a rational goal, is not found expressed before the day of Moses and the prophets, nor outside of their influence. How foreign the thought of a revelation in history was for the ancient Graeco-Roman world can be seen for example in Cicero. In his *De natura Deorum* he classifies with his usual order and particularity the forms of manifestation of divine Providence, but he does not touch

---

[16] Harald Hjärne, *Historiska världsbilder,* in *Svenskt och främmande,* pp. 147 ff.

upon or even intimate the thought of the presence of God in the events and connections of history. For Mosaism, on the other hand, the miracles of history were fundamental. God rescued his people out of Egypt. History proclaims his righteousness and grace. What differentiates the prophets and their kindred spirits from the saints and great personalities of other religions? The distinctive thing in all saints is that they have deeply experienced the love of God and revealed this for the good of man. The great men of other religions have sought and found God by fleeing *from history* into a timeless communion with God. The prophets commune with God *in history*: their inner experience becomes stronger and more rich by being filled with the thought of the work of God in history. In history they hear the voice of God. It is true, they hear other voices also. They hear the voices of a frivolous, an unrepentant, and self-sufficient people. They see arrogance and callousness, lack of understanding and darkness, so that at times everything looks dark to their eyes. They see the wrecks of fallen nations. The self-sufficient nationalism of their own people threatens to becloud every issue. The destruction of their own nation causes bitter pain, for it appears to them to be ethically conditioned and inescapable. But they know also that God lives and that he holds the reins in his hands. The identifying mark of prophetic religion, in all times, is this: God speaks to me, to us, in history, in the small history of the individual and in the great history of the nation and of the world. We need not go back to the Old Testament to find this. The greatest witness to the revelation of God in history is Jesus.

Jesus set himself as clearly as possible in dependent relation to the past history of his people, conceived of as the dealings of God with them. He came to fulfill the law and the prophets, he is the Son who follows the servants. Still more, his place in the contemporaneous history was that of a prophet.[17] Jesus did not live in the

---

[17] Einar Billing, *De etiska tankarne i urkristendomen*, Vol. II (Uppsala, 1907), pp. 6 ff. [(2nd ed.; Stockholm: Svenska kyrkans diakonistyrelses bokförlag, 1936). This was a particularly significant work and is credited with being a major impulse toward the development of an independent theology in Sweden.]

cell of the mystics. He was a champion in the midst of confusion and battle. Jesus did not stand apart on the heights as a spectator; he mingled with the crowd of human beings, although he did often withdraw to the mountain by himself alone. Jesus won his authority for every age and for every soul, not by looking away from his age and holding himself apart from its struggles, but by going deep down into the life of his people at the definite moment in which he was placed. No people has so intensively lived its history as Israel. No personality stands more firmly set in history than is Jesus. How did he not strive for his people: "Let it stand yet another year."[18] How did he not battle with his people for its soul: "How often have I desired to gather thy children!"[19] If history is not the revelation of God, the struggles of Jesus are meaningless, yea, his aim one great illusion. If you wish to have Christ you must take history with him. For he stands within history bearing the fullest measure of responsibility and under the most powerful dramatic tension.

The solidarity of Jesus with history is best shown in his anticipation of the immediate, catastrophic coming of the complete lordship of God. The transformation was at the door. No more important lesson has been learned by the theology of our day than the insight into this eschatological character of Christ's message. The kingdom was coming. Christ himself was to be revealed in the clouds of heaven coming in great glory before the end of his generation. There is nothing here to fear or to conceal. Christ expected a catastrophe which did not occur. On the contrary, his expectation of a speedy transformation belongs to the true humanity of Christ. This has in principle always been held by the church. This expectation proved itself of great significance for his calling. The eschatological tension helped to compress his demands and make them firm and essential. At the same time they were thereby lifted up to an ideal height, which makes them valid beyond his own time. The

[18] [Luke 13:8.]
[19] [Matt. 23:37.]

138

moments were precious. A weak man would have shouted, hurried, run anxiously from one thing to another, or else have given up all action, sat down with folded hands to look up into heaven and to speculate with the apocalyptists as to the nature of the coming life. The strong man was calm as never before. The concentration made for a gathered power. Jesus had no time for all the unimportant nonessentials of culture. "Your heavenly Father knoweth that ye have need of these things."[20] But he had time for all that must be done. He treated every individual case with that great conscientiousness which alone he possesses for whom the present moment is filled with eternity. His eyes caressed lovingly the flowers of the field, his teaching reached to the heart and center of the moral life. Furthermore, this eschatological expectation was no chance, passing thing. It is found also in many of the great figures of history. This is due not merely to the fact that the life of the individual is short and the end immediately at the door; not to the fact, which is psychologically true, that in the moment of the greatest concentration of life, death stands near us without causing us fear.[21]

Time remains brief when we stand before the ideal, even if millions of years spread out before humanity on its march. In the midst of labors, burdened for the future, the great personalities of history have lived in an eschatological tension. Darkness closed down upon them, but within them the goal lived as a present demand and the issue as a present reality. The goal was such that no merely human progress, however long, could fulfill its meaning,

[20] [Matt. 6:32.]

[21] This was written in 1911, a few years before the great war. The world catastrophe furnished an unexpected commentary on the eschatological and apocalyptic scriptures. Their seemingly fantastic scenes were given meaning. The little apocalypse found in the synoptics speaks of the final tribulation. Were we not already entered upon the beginning of the birthpangs? The drama of the apocalyptic was no longer merely a curiosity. It received life and content. The Book of Revelation in the New Testament won many new readers. No other passages in the Scriptures or the sacred literature of the race could better express what men felt. Before this the eschatological and apocalyptical writings needed an apologetic. Interpreters sought to soften them, to explain away their wild and varied imagery. The comfort of civilization could not tolerate such bizarre things. But when the world-anguish had ravaged us for a time, they no longer needed interpretation. Least of all could they be explained away (1930).

but the heavenly vision was very near. For them, as for Jesus, the eschatological expectation and feeling signified that beyond the thunders of history, and the angel voices too, they saw and heard what was in reality taking place, in spite of the present seeming bewilderment. The prince of this world was being cast out. The Son of man was drawing all unto himself (John 12:29-32).

Belief in the continued revelation of God has since the day of the prophets created a literature characterized by one or the other of two motives, either a gloomy turning from the present to a violent catastrophe, or a more optimistic evolutionary doctrine. What is more important, the certainty that God is really the actor in the drama of history has produced personalities which shine with the light of God. Permit me to name some of these out of the Christian world of western Europe. The church of the Middle Ages and France possesses the most beautiful of all, Jeanne d'Arc. We have already mentioned her name. Lutheranism has Luther and Gustavus Adolphus. Calvinism has Calvin and Gaspard de Coligny and Cromwell. History is indeed difficult to understand. Instead of God's great plans the pious often see only their own little ideals. Over-curious apologetics have been discredited and justly so. But the great fundamental thought remains: God reigns. It is retained by the faith of the heart, even though our dim eyes cannot clearly see the application. Most clearly have all the devoted champions of history and the historians of genuine genius apprehended it. One of their rare but weighty confessions may here be heard: "Do the laws of human progress proceed on their undisturbed march through the ages in accordance with, or contrary to, the will of the acting personalities or nations? What are these laws? No one knows their inner nature, but their results can be traced more or less clearly, if one listens attentively to the voice of the past. At times, in the manner in which events establish their own connection, we gain a glimpse of something which resembles a human face, shining with a smile both stern and mild over the nations, which although they think themselves marching in ways of their own choosing, always arrive at goals at which they did not aim. If this glimpse is an illusion, it has nevertheless awakened the surmise that the implacable laws of evolution are in reality not a system of rules of mechanism, but expressions of a personal will, against which no other can prevail. And in the center of the history of the world there arises a personality which is not like any that we know. He points forward to a goal, toward which all the devious ways of the peoples are drawn together in a peace which exceeds all their plans and dreams. Faith in Christ is a power for progress and life which since his day has ruled the world, even against its will, and which strengthens those wills which are devoted to his service."[22]

Denmark received in Grundtvig a prophetic spirit for whom history, the past, the present, and the future were the workshop of God. He interpreted the signs of the times. He advised and judged his people according to the promptings of the Spirit. He showed his people their place in the merciful providence of God. Edward Lehman has left to his own and coming generations his book[23] about Grundtvig as an inheritance which puts them in his debt. It is perhaps his most beautiful work, certainly an utterance which sets Grundtvig in the line of the prophets of all times, not merely the four major and the twelve minor prophets in Israel, but "monks and nuns from the cloisters of the North and the South, Russian peasants, English laborers, American folk preachers, highly cultivated writers, a Francis of Assisi, a St. Birgitta, a George Fox, a Joseph Smith, a Thomas Carlyle, a Dostoievski, prophets for today and for tomorrow, as for past millenniums." To show what a prophetic eye Grundtvig had for history we note the remarkable fact that the last thing which the aged man requested be read to him on the day of his death, the Fourteenth Sunday after Trinity, Septem-

[22] Harald Hjärne, *Gustaf Adolfs minne*, in *Svenskt och främmande*, pp. 55 f.
[23] [E. Lehman, *Grundtvig* (Copenhagen: Jespersen og Pios Forlag, 1929). For studies of Grundtvig in English see P. G. Lindhardt, *Grundtvig: An Introduction* (London: SPCK, 1951); Hal Koch, *Grundtvig*, trans. Llewellyn Jones (Yellow Springs, Ohio: Antioch, 1952); Johannes Knudsen, *Danish Rebel* (Philadelphia: Muhlenberg, 1955); Ernest D. Nielsen, *N.F.S. Grundtvig: An American Study* (Rock Island, Ill.: Augustana, 1955).]

ber 1, 1872, after he had returned home from the church in Vartov where he had preached, was Geijer's *The History of the Swedish People*, and *Historical Archives*. Lehman recognizes in him the true prophetic inspiration, intuition, and vision. Moreover, the vocation of judge also was given to Grundtvig. He arose, as did the prophets of Israel, and preached repentance and spoke the truth with courage. He pronounced severe judgments, as did Jeremiah, even against his own wishes, and contrary to the kindness of his heart. Love was the deep, the divine element in his nature. And yet, in spite of all, he looked into the future with unconquerable hope, through his power of inspiration and his Christian faith. He cast his eye back to the beginning of time. He looked forward to its consummation. He learned to see God's will in the saga of Denmark as well as in the history of the world as a whole. The kingdom is coming, the millennium. This seer of the Northland was a true interpreter of the apocalyptic scenes of the Book of Revelation (1930).[24]

Heaven is not closed since the days of the Bible. The Christian sees heaven open in the Bible as nowhere else, and when darkness threatens to engulf him, he turns to its pages to find the eternal light penetrating the dark shadows. God's revelation, however, continues throughout all time. Thus far we agree with Roman Catholic doctrine. At this point, however, an important difference arises. Romanism says: "God continues his revelation in an institution which culminates in the pope." We say: "God's continuing revelation is in men, in history." We too believe that the church is the creation and instrument of God. The religious significance of the church can be overrated, it is true, but it can also be underrated. God has committed to the church the divine privilege and the awful responsibility of communicating the grace of God to the world in word and deed and sacrament. Our belief in a continued revelation in history compels us to acknowledge, with greater conscientiousness and reverence than ever, the value of persons and of

[24] [This paragraph was a footnote in Söderblom's 1930 edition.]

means and of institutions with which the divine guidance has provided our churches in the ordinances of history. But the church ought to be more open-eyed than it is to the vision of God's continued revelation of himself. The Protestant doctrine that God has revealed himself pre-eminently in the Bible, and perhaps also through the sacraments, is true, and must be realized with renewed power. At the same time, it must not be forgotten that the chief lesson of the Bible itself is that God is a living God and has not grown aged or less active now than in his younger days. The Roman view finds the biblicism of the Protestant narrowminded and says: "God is in his church, he speaks through the ecclesiastical authority." At the same time that authority severs all connection with real history and buries itself in desperation in a mausoleum of antiquated thoughts and obsolete ideas.

Against the Roman doctrine we raise two objections: 1) It makes the continued revelation of God leave the ground of history and become institutionalized. 2) It permits the continued revelation of God to abandon the area of life and shuts it up in a theological system which was once alive but is now only a venerable memorial of the past. God reveals himself in history outside the church as well as inside of it. Was not Cyrus, the pagan ruler, called messiah by the prophet?[25] God reveals himself in the destiny of peoples as well as in the institutions of religion. Standing on the Acropolis with the eye gliding over the Gulf of Saronica, along the bold lines of the coast from Cape Sunium in the bend of Eleusis back of Salamis, one may ask oneself which had the greater significance for the history of the reign of God on the earth, Marathon and Salamis, where the Athenians fought for their state, or Eleusis, farthest back in the stillness of the bay, where they sought comfort against mortality? It may come to pass, one can never know, that in some situations statesmen may be of greater significance for the kingdom of God than many thousands of preachers. It is possible for a few dreaming and acting utopians to accomplish more for the purposes

[25] [Isa. 45:1.]

of God than the most glorious hierarchy or the best balanced and reputable piety, which calls those others mad. It may happen that political changes now in the Far East, the union of spiritual and material forces in a more comprehensive mutual influence and competition, the leveling of culture, such as is shown in the fact that the same curriculum is followed in the University of Shansi as in the University of Paris, the sharper competition between the great types of life going on under the surface, or again the influx of social movements in our own civilization, constitute a mightier revelation of God than any undertaking of the churches. God is able to speak to humanity even through lips which deny his existence.

These sentences of mine are not intended as paradoxes, they are meant to be taken in actual literalness. In the complex progress of events only he can see the will of God who takes his part in the struggle and feels responsibility for the values involved. Suddenly the fog may lift. He is able to make out what is taking place. There are movements of the times in which it is difficult for any Christian with an open eye not to see the work of God. Through these world movements Christianity is brought both theoretically and practically to a test. Is it alive, does it think, does it act in the presence of the living God? Or is it shut up within the cheap self-satisfactions of little cliques, in a sort of esoteric artificiality or a dead scholastic interest? Does it possess receptivity for divine influences or has it settled upon the lees of its forms, habits, impulses?

The consciousness of a divine working in history has not arisen from the contemplation of the course of events and the motive powers of civilization, but out of a central religious experience of a personal character in the prophets. Belief in a revelation lives at all times under the same conditions. Geijer found it terrible "that the conception of order will be lost if it is found possible to prove it only from material existence." It is easy to show that the fundamental idea in our civilization, namely, *evolution*, comes out of the biblical revelation on which our civilization thus lives, however far removed the optimism of our modern enthusiasts for evolution may be from the judgment proclamations of the prophets. It is clearly evident that philosophic thought concerning the events and progress of the world, if it proceeds from materialistic premises, invariably lands us in the doctrine of eternal cycles. This is true of our own philosophy as well as of that of other cultures.

The amiable heroes of civilization, or shall we say slaves of civilization who believe that they can reject the fundamental biblical idea of revelation and yet rejoice in progress, are guilty of a happy inconsistency. There are those also who deny, theoretically, the authority of the prophets and yet are true successors of the prophets, for they sincerely and unselfishly exert their powers for the betterment of the world in the future. A sufficiently far-sighted and thorough-going analysis of culture can with difficulty escape the insight that the only thing which gives, or can give, a soul to the restless body of Western education and technique and save our civilization, with its strivings, from self-contradiction and self-destruction is the certainty that existence in its reality is will, creative will, with a revelation and a way of life founded upon that certainty. However, just as such an insight in its historical beginning in the prophets of Israel and in Zoroaster—we have no proofs of any earlier origin—did not arise out of speculation about human culture and history, but out of the personal mysticism of communion with God, so at all times its origin must be in personalities who have religiously and historically lived themselves into and retained in an effective way this certainty. It does not have its foundation in conclusions drawn from the outward course of events and from the conditions of culture, but rather in the conflicts and victories of the inner personal life. Humanity must through anguish of soul and by the attraction of spiritual power, be forced *out* of history and civilization, and must feel the power of God in order to learn to see the revelation of God *in* history.

III

From the men of creative genius and from history we now pass to the third area of the continued revelation of God, the re-creation of the individual human being. What is the essential significance of the fact that a person becomes a Christian? We answer, two things. First, that a creation takes place within him, something original manifests itself in him in a measure analogous to the emergence of genius. Second, that he consciously enters into the historical progress of revelation.

1. God creates something new in the individual life. We have caught a glimpse of that mysterious continuation of the process of creation which reveals itself in men of unique endowment. But in men and women of only ordinary powers something can happen which is akin to the phenomenon of genius. The resemblance does not consist in any peculiar intuitive or ecstatic working of the mind. In any case this is not the essential likeness. On the whole we must guard against giving peculiar and unusual psychical manifestations a value which they only apparently possess. The resemblance consists in the results achieved, that something relatively new and original emerges. This consists in a new freedom which is won through the complete subordination under the will of God. Ethical independence, the spiritual individuality, the "new man," is no more made according to prescription than the work of genius is produced according to a ready-made rule. In the "new man" there appears a life that is raised above nature and possesses its principle within itself. When a man, heartbroken and repentant, turns resolutely from sin; when a soul in sincerity throws itself on the condemning and redeeming mercy of God; when a person, in spite of compulsion, temptation or calculation simply does his duty; when he concentrates himself in wholehearted prayer; when in temptation and confusion clarity wins the victory; when personality vindicates its freedom, then, in that sacred hour, there is produced a new crea-

tion. In conversion, in the birth to a new life, when truth, with sincerity and without sentimental softness, is reckoned with in the inner life, the soul is lifted by the power of God to the heights of moral life and of communion with God, to a life which in its newness is akin to genius. I quote with pleasure the words of Kierkegaard, that life is a poem which we ourselves are to write, but the Christian allows God to write his life's poem for him.

How essential moral independence is for Christianity is evident, among other facts, in its acknowledged relation to the most intimate and unfailing religious mark of Christian piety, namely, the prayer of the heart. The specific proof of genuine answer to prayer, real prayer, not simply suggestion by means of psychological or mechanical methods, has traditionally been found in the fact that God has been revealed, not only in a certain emotional mood, but in a new power to overcome sin and difficulty. The great men of prayer in Christendom have not been content to make a sense of increased vital power in favorable conditions the ethical criterion of answer to prayer, nor rest from weariness, nor powers of concentration in the midst of division and confusion. They have found it rather in the fact that prayer has brought them strength in the struggle against satanic temptations, peace of mind enabling them to work in the midst of storming attack, bitter misunderstanding, and terrible misfortunes; in the experience of quiet trust when spirit and body have been vexed, and in great spiritual rewards through suffering. No truth has found a clearer expression in modern times than the truth that moral independence belongs to the essence of Christianity. Kant is in this matter the authoritative interpreter of the gospel. It is incontrovertible that, whether we condemn or approve, we find in the Kantian doctrine of the majesty and absoluteness of the ethical demand the product, or rather the fulfillment, of the metaphysical ground of the Christian ethic. Kant's poverty-stricken *Religion within the Limits of Pure Reason* is at one point profound and wonderful. In the presence of the fundamental fact of the moral life Kant bows in the dust and worships. There, without hesitation, he yields absolute reverence and obedience. Wilhelm Herrmann has moved away from Kant and yet maintained the same direction. He has taken the final step. He has not paused in the purely formal absoluteness of the demand of conscience. He leads the soul on to Christ, in whom the demand receives a concrete content which judges and puts man to death just so long as he thinks himself able to care for himself in his own strength, but which brings about a divine creation in him, namely, trust in the mercy of God, so soon as he permits God to take him by the hand.

When we thus, from certain points of view, draw a parallel between the ethical liberation of the individual and the phenomenon of creative genius,[26] this does not mean that we fail to appreciate the fact that the moral life holds a unique place as compared with that which is merely natural or produced by culture only, or as compared with certain other elements in human life which are expressions only of a highly gifted personality. Actually there is an essential difference between a personal life animated from within by a spiritual and moral renewal, and a human existence which lacks such a point of departure exalted above mere nature. This difference may be established by observing the hierarchies of life accessible to us. Nevertheless, the moral life, when we find it exalted above mere legality or customary morality into personal independence, reveals striking analogies to the creation of genius. In the case of both, in the moral character as well as in genius, there is at hand a norm, not in the shape of outward rule but as an inward principle, the working of which cannot be determined beforehand but which, in its every function, constitutes its own rule, and when it comes to expression reveals a cohesion and a beauty in accordance with its peculiar variety of life. To consider the norm as being merely a pattern in accordance with which something is formed, is to misinterpret the creative power of genius and the

[26] A masterly description of the power of spiritual awakening to lift a human being out of ordinary powers into a higher existence is given from actual life in Selma Lagerlöf's *A Fallen King.*

essential being of the personal life as well. This inner principle, of the work of art or of the ethical personality, manifests itself in both as absolute, as a compulsion which is not like that of instinct or of some outward restraint that enslaves, degrades, and finally destroys that unity of personality which is a mark of the mature ethical person. It is rather an absolute compulsion which, when obeyed, either in the fire of genius as it creates or in the labors and decisions of the life of conscience, conquers, exalts, and confirms freedom and inner unity. This absolute compulsion of an inner principle reveals a third point of similarity. In both there is the common mark of life that it is a continuing creation which constantly brings forth that which is new. Even in the primitive stages of religion the initiation into the mysteries of the tribe means that the young initiate is held to have died and been born again into a new and higher life, so that he is in reality "twice-born." The endlessly varying symbolism of death and resurrection to a higher life found in the terminology of the mystery cults and religion receives a new and more definite and noteworthy meaning when it is applied to moral renewal. "The new man" is more than a mere figure of speech. It is a revelation of the upward striving of the process of creation.

2. The Christianity of the individual signifies further that revelation continues its history in him. He finds that his life means a choice between alternatives. Shall the creative power of God or shall the destructive power of evil rule his inner life? The movement of the great world drama seizes upon the individual soul. No neutrality is possible in the tremendous contradiction between life and death, creation or ruin. Every human soul must take its part in the struggle. At the same time the individual is made a part of that history of revelation which has already transpired. The history of God's dealings in the past becomes a history of God's present dealing with that particular soul. This history of the past becomes his own present history. "It happened for me." "Given and shed for you"—the most important event in the life of the individual is Jesus Christ. Not only so. Everything which takes place in the little

history of the individual soul finds a new meaning; it becomes the dealing of God with his child.

Herein lies the Christian conception of *miracle*. An event in the outer or it may be in the inner life takes place. Or some person is found to constitute in a measure a divine revelation, and as such is seen to belong to a higher world than that of cause and effect as established by science. For the so-called primitive view, as well as for paganism and for remainders of ancient thought still surviving in our Christian civilization, miracle is that which we cannot understand. For Christian faith miracle is the opposite; it is, namely, that which faith really understands. We must examine this essential difference a little more closely. A man dies. No arrow struck him, no lion killed him, no waters drowned him. For the primitive man the case is one of mystery, magic, witchcraft; a powerful, mysterious, and dangerous force or will must have been involved in the matter. On a higher plane of culture events and phenomena are connected together in a comprehensive system, but essentially the same attitude of mind may continue. An amazing happening, an unusual case, a fact that cannot be explained, is ascribed to a direct action by a spirit or god or to the supernatural powers of some man, and thus becomes a miracle. The mind of antiquity held a miracle to be a wonder—that which was unexplained or could not be explained. "Miracle is that which awakens amazement, whether it rises above nature or not" (Forcellini). The miraculous was the same as the strange, a prodigy, an omen, a fearful mystery, that which by its magnitude or its beauty awakens amazement.

Church writers gave the word a special meaning by reason of the dominating conception of God. Miracle was for them that which exceeded the powers of created nature, or that which happened contrary to the usual order and which is originated by God alone. This ecclesiastical conception held that the essential thing in a miracle was that it was inexplicable in the order of nature. This natural-historical point of view dominated in spite of the Christian idea of God, or at least it was of equal force with the religious idea. This is evident, characteristically, in the definitions of St. Thomas Aquinas which, essentially, have been retained by evangelical scholasticism. In his *Summa Theologica*[27] he defines the concept miracle as "that which happens outside of the order of nature known to us, in which sense God alone can work miracles." If the wonderful event does not fall outside of the area of nature, although it exceed our knowledge, it is a miracle only for us, but not in itself (*quoad nos, sed non simpliciter*). In his apologetic work *Summa contra Gentiles* or *Summa philosophica*,[28] St. Thomas differentiates in the same way between that which is simply marvellous, *simpliciter mirum*, the cause of which may be hidden from one person and known to another, and the miracle, the cause of which is known to no human being in this life, for it is of God and not of nature. "By miracle then is meant that which is wrought by God, outside the general order of things."[29] The dominating point of view in this definition also is the negative one, namely, that man cannot grasp the cause, for it is God and not nature.

This dualism of God and nature, of the Creator and his creation, is still more marked in the three grades of miracles indicated by St. Thomas. The highest grade is that miracle in which God does something which nature never can do, as when two bodies occupy the same space, or the sun goes backward or stands still, or a path appears in the sea by which we may cross it. The next grade is that miracle in which God works that which nature also can do, but not in the same order, as when a creature lives after death, receives his sight after blindness, etc. The third and lowest grade is that miracle in which God does that which nature is wont to do but without using the powers of nature, as when one is healed of a curable sickness by divine power, or when it rains without the ordinary working of nature. The miracle therefore consists in the fact that God acts, setting aside the causal order which he has insti-

[27] Part I, qu. 110, art. 4.
[28] Bk. III, chap. 101.
[29] *Illa igitur simpliciter miracula dicenda sunt quae divinitus fiunt praeter ordinem communiter servatum in rebus.*

tuted and which constitutes the created order of nature. God is present in the causal order as its ultimate cause, whereas in the miracle he suspends those causes which are near at hand and accessible to our knowledge, and intervenes directly, without their mediation.

Augustine produced another doctrine of miracle out of his Platonic premises. For him everything was practically equally miraculous, for the all-penetrating creative power of God is everywhere present. For man, however, certain unusual events, proceeding from the eternal resources of God, are miracles. They cannot, indeed, be contradictory of nature, for nature is the work of God himself. The contradiction lies in our own understanding, which is limited to the usual processes of nature.

The conception of miracle held by St. Thomas, under the influence of the Aristotelian world view, with its antithesis between the created causal order and the intervention of God as prompted by his government of the universe, gained precedence as the orthodox view of the church and found its final expression in the conception of miracle as the temporary suspension of nature's laws. This conception of miracle makes of it something which is fundamentally indifferent ethically and religiously. This is not so clearly seen in the stricter conception of miracles held by the Scholastics, in which miracle lies outside of the possibilities of nature and is reserved for God alone. It is more clearly evident in their wider conception of miracle, according to which even the devil works wonders. Of course the religious point of view is not altogether lacking, as when Augustine differentiates between that which merely arouses surprise (*ludicra*) and that which results in great good (*utilia*), or when the Scholastics differentiate between the amazing work of the devil and the miracles of God, the latter of which aim at the confirmation of the truth[30] and the salvation of men. The miracle belongs to the divine government of the world. Even in this conception, however, the religious significance is not permitted to break through the ancient natural view.

This had, however, been done long before in the Bible, already

[30] See, e.g., J. Gerhard, *Systema, De ecclesia,* sec. XI.

even in those books and sayings of the Old Testament which are saturated with the spirit of Mosaism and prophetism, for which miracle has the meaning of acts of God for the purpose of salvation. It is true that the view of revealed religion is sometimes fused with the primitive, popular conception of miracles, yet it is dominating throughout, and not seldom it emerges in its purity. The place of honor is held by the marvellous works done in times of old, with similar ones in the history of the people both before and after the Exile, so long as the religious spirit possessed sufficient spiritual sensitiveness or there were personalities to interpret these events. But events in the individual or social life, also, yes, in all that God has done, in nature as well as in the law,[31] are miracles for him whose eyes have been opened to see the work of God. The fundamental idea of the biblical religions is not cult or piety, but revelation. In the New Testament, the "mighty" works of Jesus are done in his vocation, in the service of love and the rule of God, in contrast to "signs and wonders." In that strictly supernatural view which marks Christianity, God's work and God's world as a whole are miracles, if in them there is revealed the gracious will of God. This will of God, not that of phenomenal causes, is the true world order. Thus for revealed religion miracle is not that which cannot be understood, not that which merely arouses wonder, but rather that which only faith understands. In the measure that faith is conscious of the presence of God and sees a divine purpose in that which is happening, the event is unveiled as a miracle and viewed as a revelation.[32] E. G. Geijer wrote to Fredrika Bremer on November 9, 1842: "We say a miracle, not in the sense of the inexplicable, but in the sense of that which is explicable only through itself." "That it is not ignorance which makes the miracle is best shown in this, that investigation does not remove the miraculous in it, but rather brings it to the consciousness with the sense of reality."

Much, perhaps we may say most, of all that happens in nature

[31] Ps. 19. Cf. E. Billing quoted above [n. 17 of this chapter].
[32] Cf. N. J. Göransson, *Gudsförhållandets kristologiska grund* (Uppsala: Almquist & Wiksells, 1910), II, 100 ff.

and human life is either without interest to us, or is obscure and puzzling, or even tempts us to doubt and mistrust. It is possible that there is really nothing mysterious in all these happenings. The causal connection is possibly as clear and natural and commonplace as can be. Or it may still be true that, for scientific explanation, real difficulties are to be found in these events. For faith, however, they are dead, meaningless, or puzzling, disturbing. Faith cannot find in them a spiritual connection. Faith does not understand in them a purpose of God. The event may be strange, it may awaken questioning and prompt investigation, but it is no miracle in the religious sense. Where faith speaks of miracle, there faith is at home, there it understands and knows that God has done this for the salvation of man, to give aid and comfort to those who are concerned. The event in question may constitute an everlasting problem for science, as does, for example, the person of Jesus, or the origins of Christianity. Or again the event may be the most natural thing in the world, a happening in some individual life, unimportant for others, momentous for him who experiences it. From the religious point of view, the event is full of meaning and content, for here God meets man, God is making himself known to humanity or to the individual. This meeting with God belongs to the world of the inner life, yet it is bound up with history, finds its analogy chiefly with the appearing of Christ. Science must take note of it. It finds perhaps, that such a miracle or revelation-element, which has become so significant, yes, revolutionary, for the outward formation of life and history, belongs to a mighty kingdom of reality. It would be an insult to science as well as to religion should we seek to apply the religious interpretation instead of the natural or scientific. Religion moves in a deeper region of reality. Its miracles do not mean simply a temporary break in the causal chain. The religious miracle is something positive, God's action, not something negative, the unintelligible.

For Christ all was miracle; that is, he saw the work of God everywhere. Nothing was for him dead or meaningless. The heroes and saints of Christendom also have been able to see the hand of God and have fellowship with the divine, where the ordinary man thoughtless and blind, has walked unseeing through the very miracles of God all about him.

The difference between the general science of religion and Christian theology is this, that for the latter, faith in revelation is essential. For Christian theology, the history of religion is at the same time a divine self-disclosure. The general science of religion leaves the question of revelation open. A scholar may be animated by the conviction that behind the phenomena of religion lies a supra-mundane reality; or, he may deny that which is fundamental for religion, namely, faith in a spiritual reality; or, he may stand questioning and uncertain about revelation, perhaps certain only of the impossibility of knowing anything about it; or, he may lack interest entirely in the question of the truth of religion. Naturally different attitudes toward the idea of revelation must not be allowed to influence the method of scientific investigation in historical and psychological inquiries, so that these come to be distorted by dogmatism one way or the other. The cure for such mistakes cannot lie in the prohibition of any conviction on the part of the investigator. It lies simply in the correct aim of the investigation, conscientious precision and seriousness in the process, and in the readiness of the scientific spirit to bow before the actual fact.

In the biblical faith in revelation there is indeed included the conviction that one part of the history of religion constitutes revelation in a more real and a richer sense than in the history of religions in general. This doctrine of a special revelation must, however, be tested in the light of historical reality. So much can be established by a sufficiently thorough orientation, that the claim of a special revelation within the general revelation, which is made by the biblical faith, answers to that special type of religion which we have called, in the terminology of Usener, revealed religion. With this term we have not meant to express any view of the metaphysical problem concerning divine self-disclosure. We simply verify the

155

historical and psychological peculiarity of the prophetic, or personal, or vocational religions. This type of religion, revealed religion, is traced back to the special psychological conditions mentioned in the second chapter, and possesses the peculiar quality set forth in the first chapter.[33] The characteristic and essential difference between this religion and the conceptions of the ancient world in general may be clearly recognized by a cultural-historical analysis today, in such modern lines of thought as are consciously or unconsciously continuations of revealed religion.[34]

But if the Christian faith has thus marked off a certain area as belonging to special revelation, and this, to a certain extent, is analogous to that which the science of religion does when it marks off revealed religion as a unique type within the history of religion, this does not mean that the distinction is an absolute one in time and space. Neither does the science of religion do away with the fact of the affinity of all religion, when it separates them for scientific study. Actually this connection of all forms of religion into unitary groups of phenomena answers to the prophetic and Christian faith

[33] Henri Bergson had accepted two years before the World War an invitation by the Olaus Petri Foundation to deliver a series of lectures at the University of Uppsala. This brought about a correspondence concerning the theme of these lectures, which were to treat of the application of his fundamental philosophical tenets as to history and man, more especially his theory of "creative evolution." I asked him if he knew of any connection between this and the prophetic conception of history. For everywhere except in the religion of the prophets or in revealed religion history becomes fundamentally meaningless, a repetition of the same things, sin and misery, and a savior for different epochs, which, in what one might call an astronomic vastness, follow one upon another in the ancient cosmology of the Hindus, with parallels in the thought of Greece and of China. A goal for history and for progress of the world is found only in the prophetism of the Old and New Testaments from which the creations of Islam and Zoroaster have inherited the conception of purpose in the world. Bergson answered that he did not know of this connection but the thought appealed to him and he would make a closer examination of it. When the eminent disciple of Bergson, Professor Jacques Chevalier, visited Uppsala last year, the conversation centered on the postulates of Bergson's philosophy. I mentioned to him my surmise. I received the answer that a prominent French critic had discovered that Bergson was Jewish in his doctrine. The critic's opinion testifies to a correct orientation. For the conception that reality, being, is symbolized by such terms as purpose, will, creation, realization, penetration, progress, power, energy, life, has its source in the religion of the prophets (1930).

[34] Cf. my *Religionsproblemet*, II, 235 ff., 415 ff., and for the question of the portals of religion, *ibid.*, pp. 258 ff.

in a divine self-disclosure to the nations outside "the chosen people" or the influence of Christianity. In other writings I have sought to show that there is a Christian faith in a divine influence even outside the area of special revelation, in different nations and cultures. Wherein the element of revelation in any particular form of religion consists, is difficult to say; it becomes impossible if one attempts to apply an intellectualistic view. But the *fact* that there is a measure of revelation, that is, of a divine self-disclosure, wherever there is found a sincere religiousness, is expressed by faith in a revelation, which it held both within and without the Christian religion.[35]

In the foregoing pages the attempt has been made to indicate the universal application of faith in revelation, as regards time. As surely as the Christian faith holds that the divine self-impartation lies open before us, valid and inexhaustible for all time—in the sacred history and above all in the personality of Christ—equally impossible is it to hold fast to faith in revelation without extending it beyond the times of the Bible. Naturally it has been possible only to sketch the outlines here. To attempt a detailed map of the continued revelation is difficult. One incurs danger of profanation or of subjectivism. It is desirable and necessary, however, that this conviction of a continuing revelation be filled with a concrete content and that we try to interpret its meaning.

The three essential elements which have been presented, namely, genius, history, and the spiritual personality, constitute in my opinion the most important points of view for classification in the history of religion as a whole. The phenomenon of monotheism is not such a point of view. This may more often be a striving after unity in the theoretical study of religions, or of political life, rather than of religious movement. Nor is the general progress of morals more promising. This progress certainly does proceed with reciprocal influence from and upon religion, but it is by no means identified with the development of religion. These elements are concerned

[35] *Ibid.,* pp. 445 ff., 454 ff.

with 1) the fact that religion, on various stages and in various senses, is bound up with a hero, a savior and a prophet, more especially a divine personality working in the world, whether it be a deified man or a humanized, mythical creation, or a Christ; 2) the relation of religion to history; and 3) the place of the ethical values within the conception of salvation and all acts of worship and work, of life itself.

INDEX

INDEX

Ahura-Mazda, *see* Zoroaster
Andrae, T., 11, 16
Augustine, 42, 90, 103
Aulén, G., 4, 9, 10, 13, 14, 26, 27, 29, 30

Bergendoff, C., 9
Bergson, H., 156
Biblical criticism, 15
Billing, E., 4, 9, 13, 19, 20, 29, 137, 153
Boström, C. J., 79
Brilioth, Y., 14
Bring, R., 30

Carlson, E. M., 4
Carlyle, 18, 129
Christ
  as authority, 84-85, 112-115, 122, 123
  passion of, 26-27
  Sermon on the Mount, 6
Church, 19-20
Conscience, 107, 109-112
Consciousness of infinity, 107
Conversion, 146-147
Culture religions, 16-17, 45-51

Deissmann, A., 7
De Jong, K. H. E., 62
Delitzsch, F., 15
Dualism, 24, 75-78, 117-119, 151

Eckman, J. A., 7
Ecstasy, 78-79, 95
Ecumenical churchman, 3
Epictetus, 42, 43
Erasmus, 14, 25
Eschatology, 69-71
Ethics, 40, 86-87
Eucken, R., 41, 50
Evolutionary hypothesis, 16, 60

Faith, nature of, 105-107
Fehr, F., 85
Ferré, N., 4

Geijer, E. G., 79, 95, 128, 153
Geismar, E., 40
Genius, 122, 124-136
Gottschick, J., 135
Grundtvig, 141
Gunkel, H., 42, 55

Harnack, A., 7, 91

Type: Body, 11 on 13 and 10 on 11 Garamond
Display, Garamond
Paper: 'R' Antique

SEMINAR EDITIONS

Philip Jacob Spener, *Pia Desideria.* Translated, edited, and with an Introduction by Theodore G. Tappert.

Martin Kähler, *The So-Called Historical Jesus and the Historic, Biblical Christ.* Translated, edited, and with an Introduction by Carl E. Braaten.

Samuel Simon Schmucker, *Fraternal Appeal to the American Churches, with a Plan for Catholic Union on Apostolic Principles.* Edited and with an Introduction by Frederick K. Wentz.

Vilhelm Beck, *Memoirs.* A Story of Renewal in the Denmark of Kierkegaard and Grundtvig. Edited and with an Introduction by Paul C. Nyholm. Translated by C. A. Stub.

Nathan Söderblom, *The Nature of Revelation.* Edited and with an Introduction by Edgar M. Carlson. Translated by Frederic E. Pamp.

In Preparation: Volumes from the writings of Johann Hinrich Wichern, Eric Norelius, Wilhelm Loehe, Ludwig Ihmels, C. F. W. Walther, and others.

44603

231.74
So 1

Date Due

4/14/65	DEC 2 '75		
MAY 29 '8	APR 4 '78		
7/12/69	MAR 15 '79		
NOV 3	MAR 10 1982		
NOV 1 7 '70			
JAN 4 71	AP 3 3 02		
OCT 22 '74			
NOV 5 '74			
NOV 26 '74			
NOV 26 '74			
APR 29 75			